"Beyond the Trees"

a mosaic mural by

Josef Norris

and

Kid Serve Youth Muralists

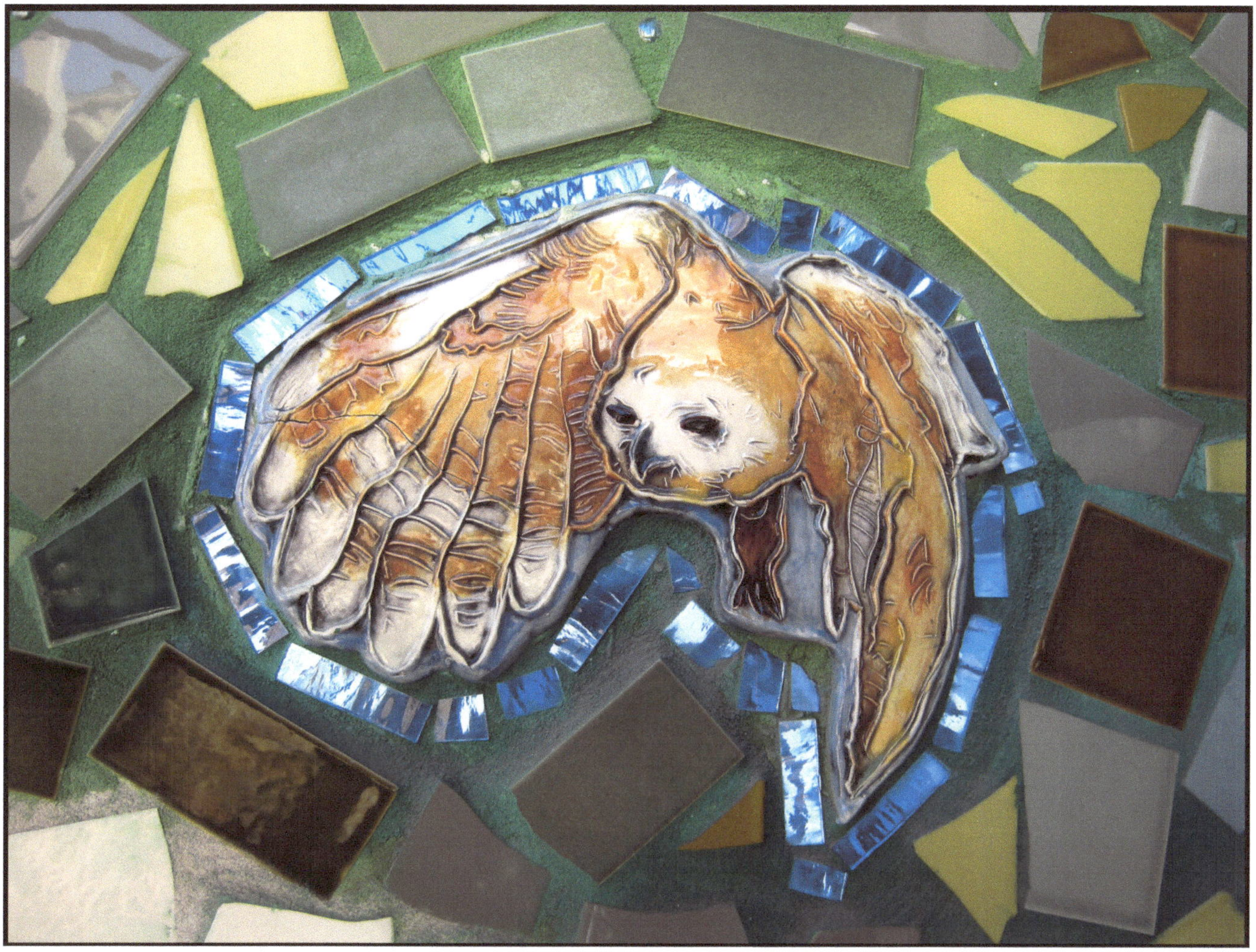

by Josef Norris

Kid Serve Books

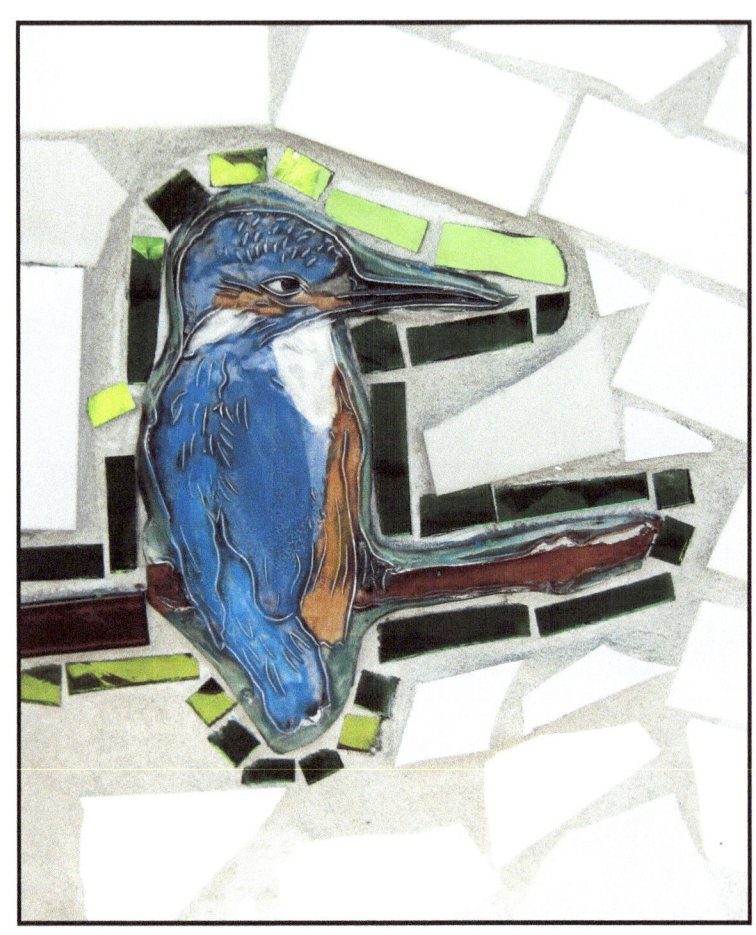

Beyond the Trees

By Josef Norris

Cover: "Beyond the Trees" at 170 Otis Street in San Francisco 2010

Back: Detail from "Beyond the Trees" 2010

First edition, 2010

Text and Photographs © 2010
By Josef Norris
www.josefnorris.com
www.kidserve.com

Published by Kid Serve Books
1068 Bowdoin Street
San Francisco, CA 94134

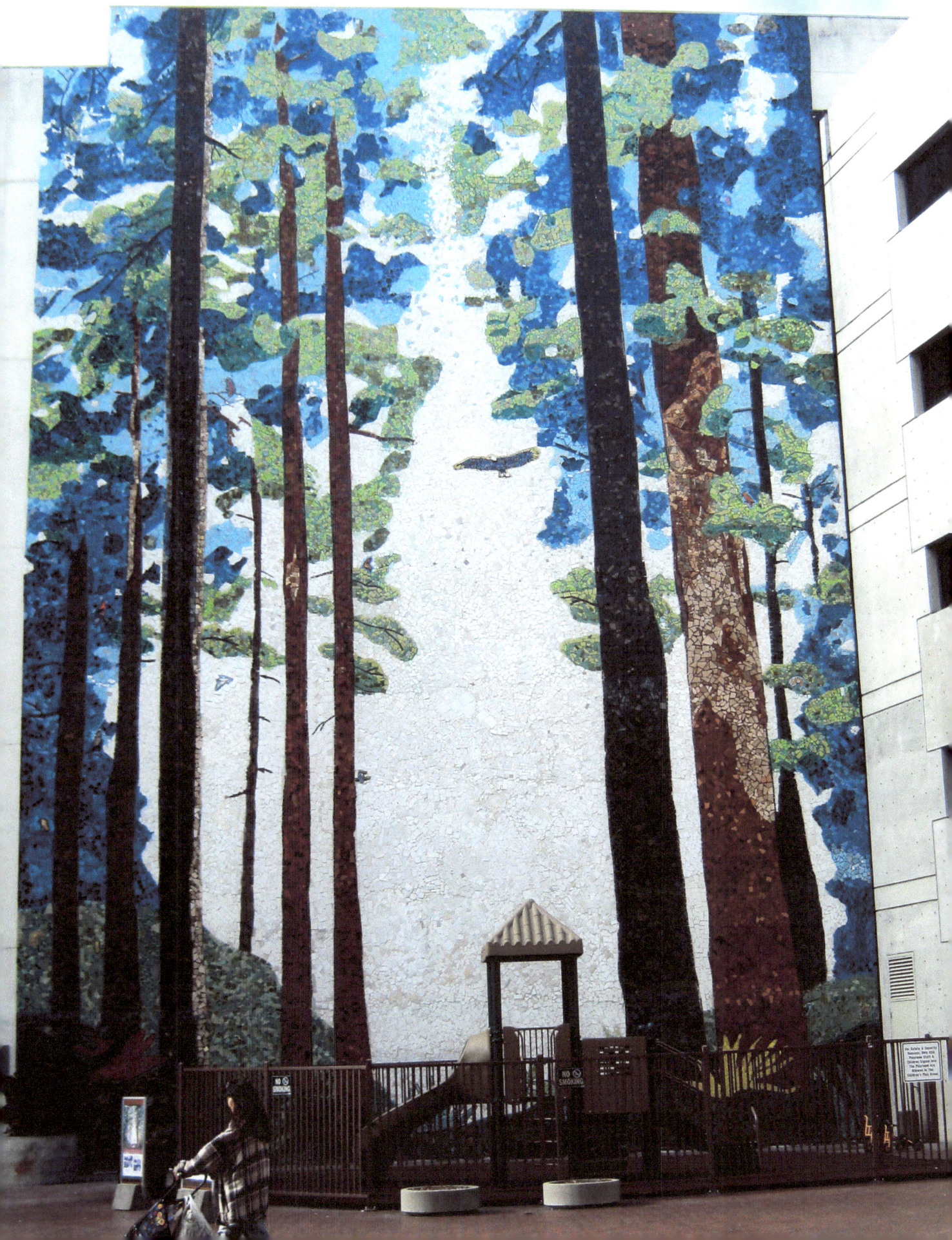

In the summer of 2010 I joined with a group of 35 foster youth at San Francisco's Independent Living Skills Program to create what would become one of the largest mosaic murals in North America. We built a 6-story mosaic mural of a redwood forest towering over a play structure at the entrance Human Services Agency in San Francisco. The goal was to completely transform the space.

The project began in 2008. I had a site visit with Michele Rutherford of the San Francisco Human Services Agency. As we looked at the 170 Otis Plaza, surrounded on three sides by 6-story poured concrete, we both agreed that the entrance looked very "institutional". I have many "look and see" site visits every year and normally they never materialize. This project was different. Michele kept calling me back. I kept having meetings with the Human Services staff and we developed a vision for how we could do a large-scale project involving San Francisco foster youth. When I reached out to funders and individual donors, I found them to be very eager to support a public art project with this population of young people.

During that first meeting I noticed that there were two large trees at the front gates of the plaza. An architect or building contractor had made a conscious effort to keep those trees. Those trees became my inspiration for the image of redwood forest.

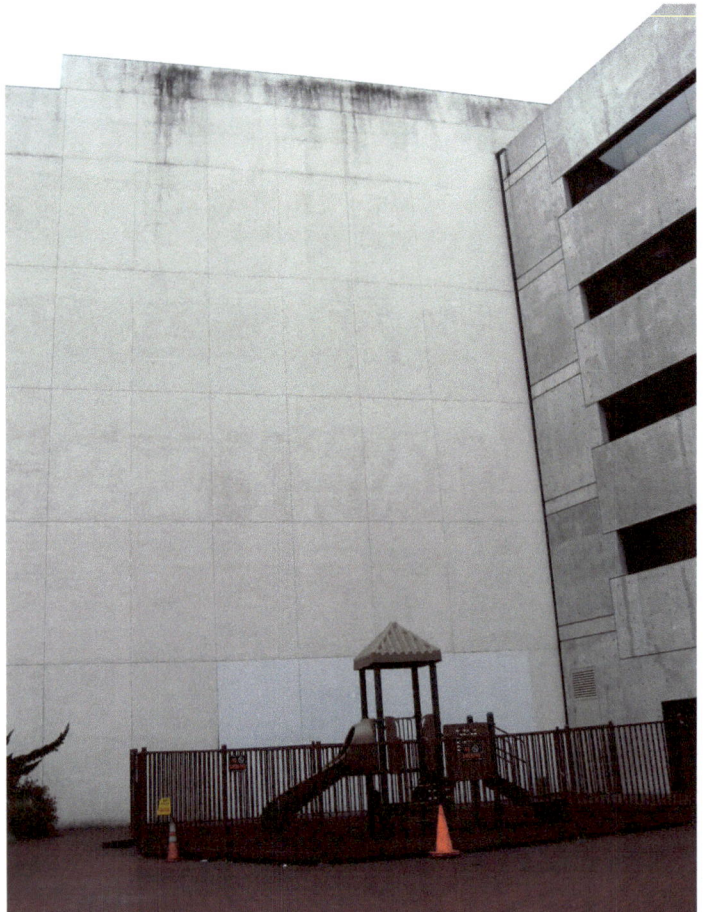

170 Otis Street in 2009.

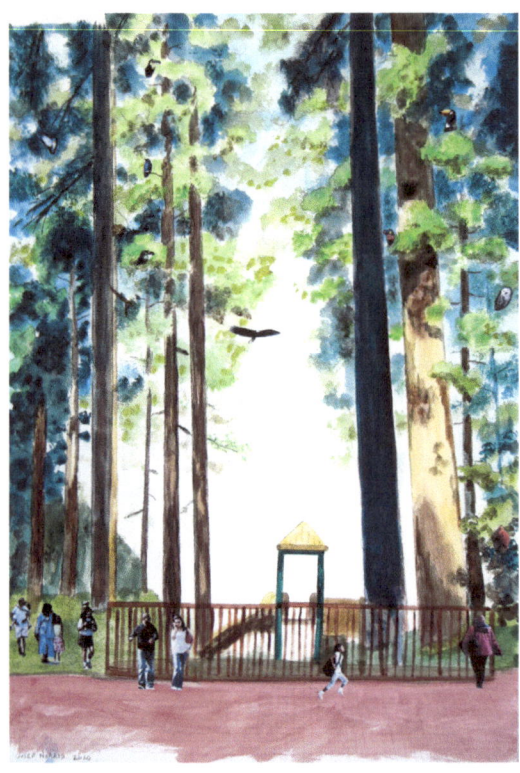

The final design for "Beyond the Trees".

Building the mural in the studio

In May of 2010, Atalanta Powell and I started work on the top 40 feet of the mural. We started by laying out thick plastic sheeting and making a 40' high ink drawing of the forest. We then painted on the back side of the plastic. Adding color to the plastic sections would help when working with numerous young artists in a classroom setting.

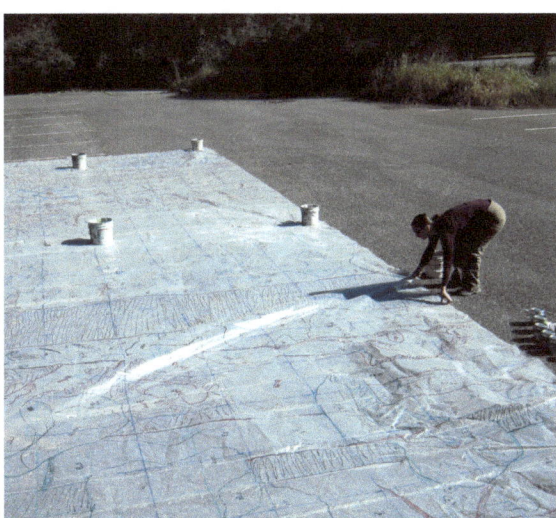 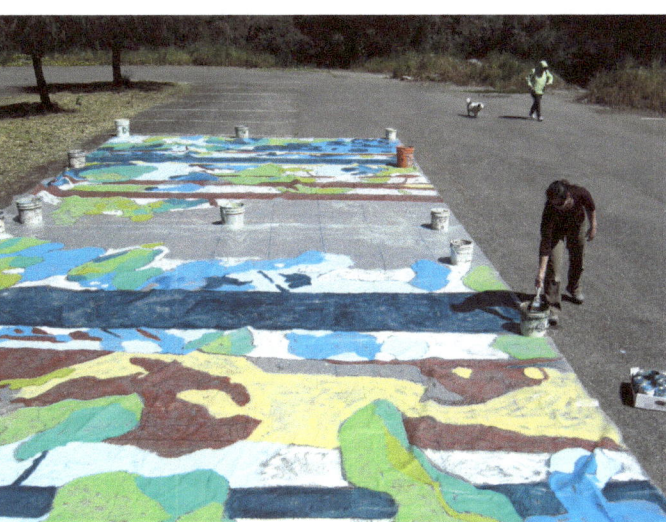

We then cut and numbered the plastic pieces and attached custom fitted nylon mesh on to them, in essence making a 40' high x 50' wide jigsaw puzzle. For two months our crew headed by Atalanta Powell and Delaine Hackney, built the top part of the mural in the studio. Because we were building an image that was so immense and large – it felt like we were working blind. I was cautiously optimistic that the mural would look like the intended design. But I couldn't be sure until it was up on the wall.

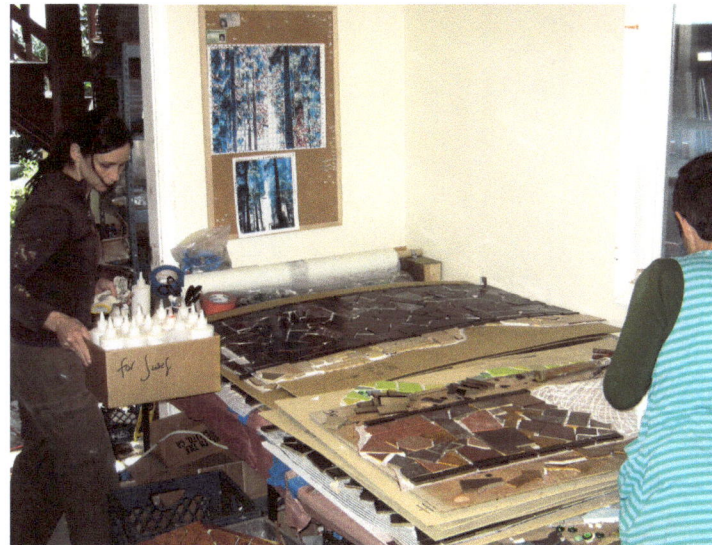

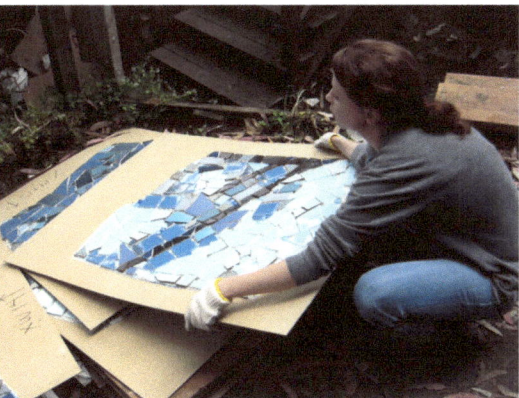

Angela Baker organizing the 500 giant mosaic pieces at the end of June 2010.

Atalanta Powell and Delaine Hackney building sections of the mural in the studio.

Starting in mid July we began working with foster youth at the Independent Living Skills Program in San Francisco to help build sections of the giant mosaic mural. We had an exceptional group of young people working with us.

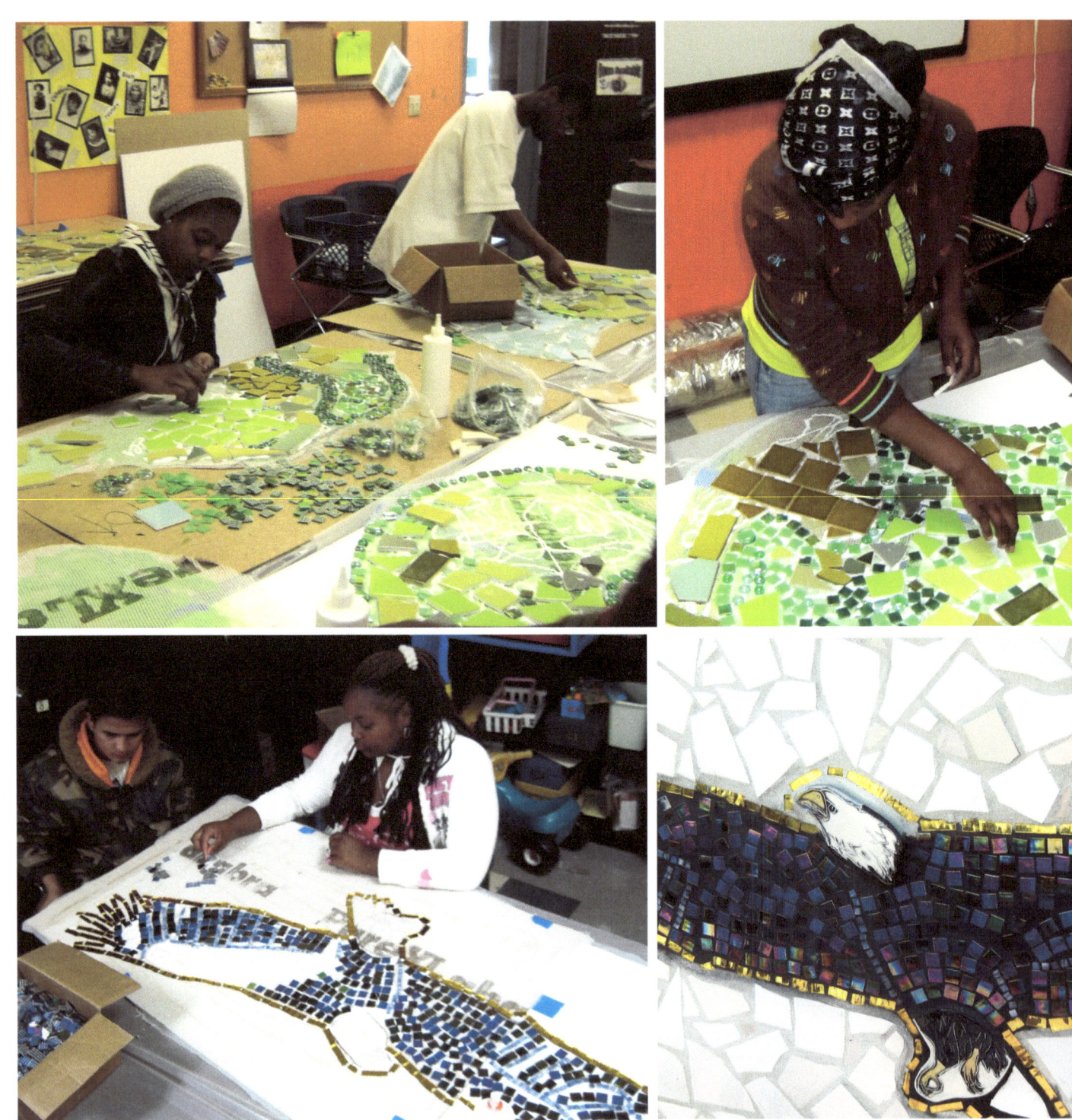

The artists built sections of the mosaic mural on nylon mesh. These pieces were then installed throughout the mural.

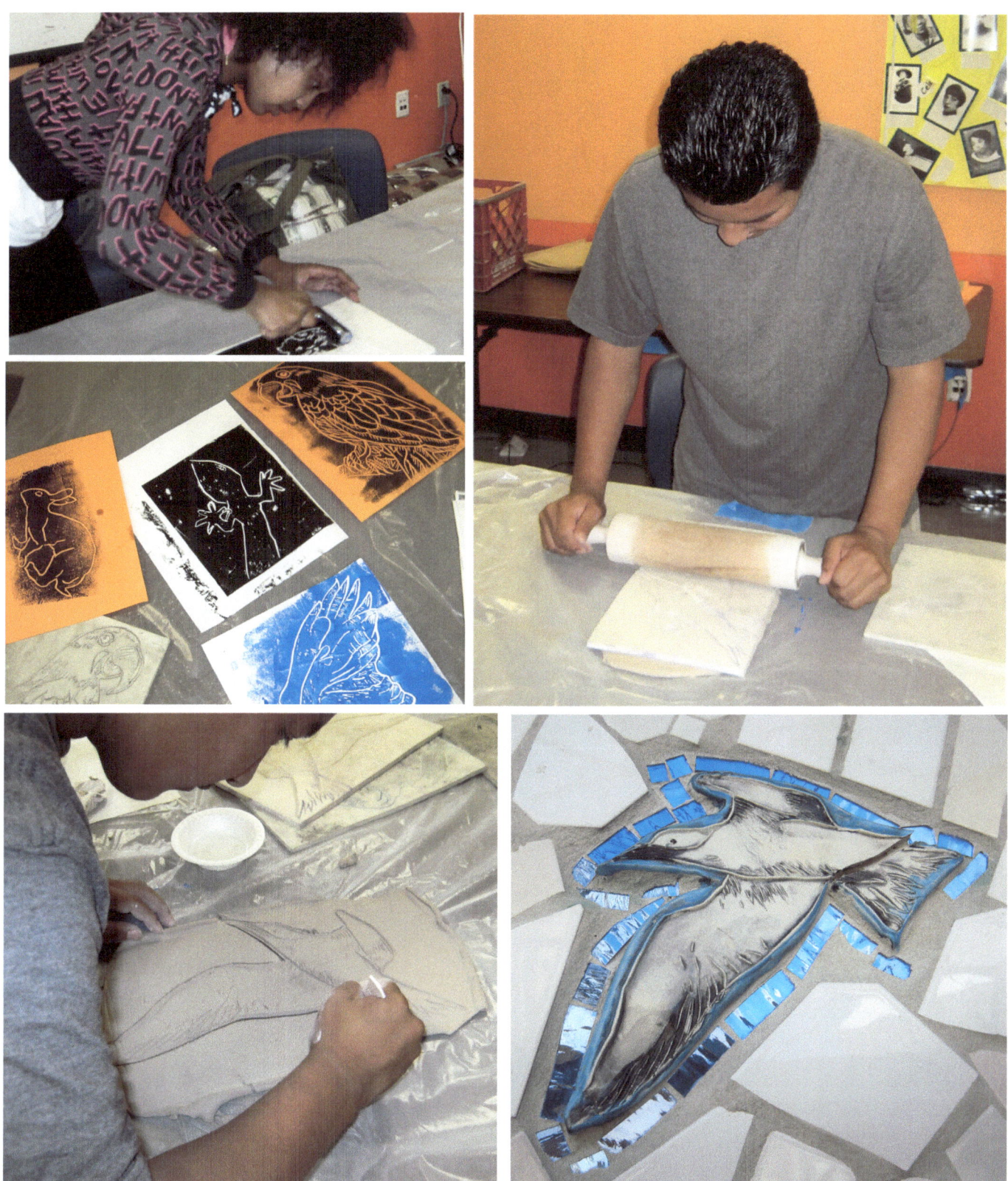

The young artists created linoleum block cuts of exotic birds and used those to make ceramic imprints. After they were glazed and fired, they were installed throughout the mural by our crew.

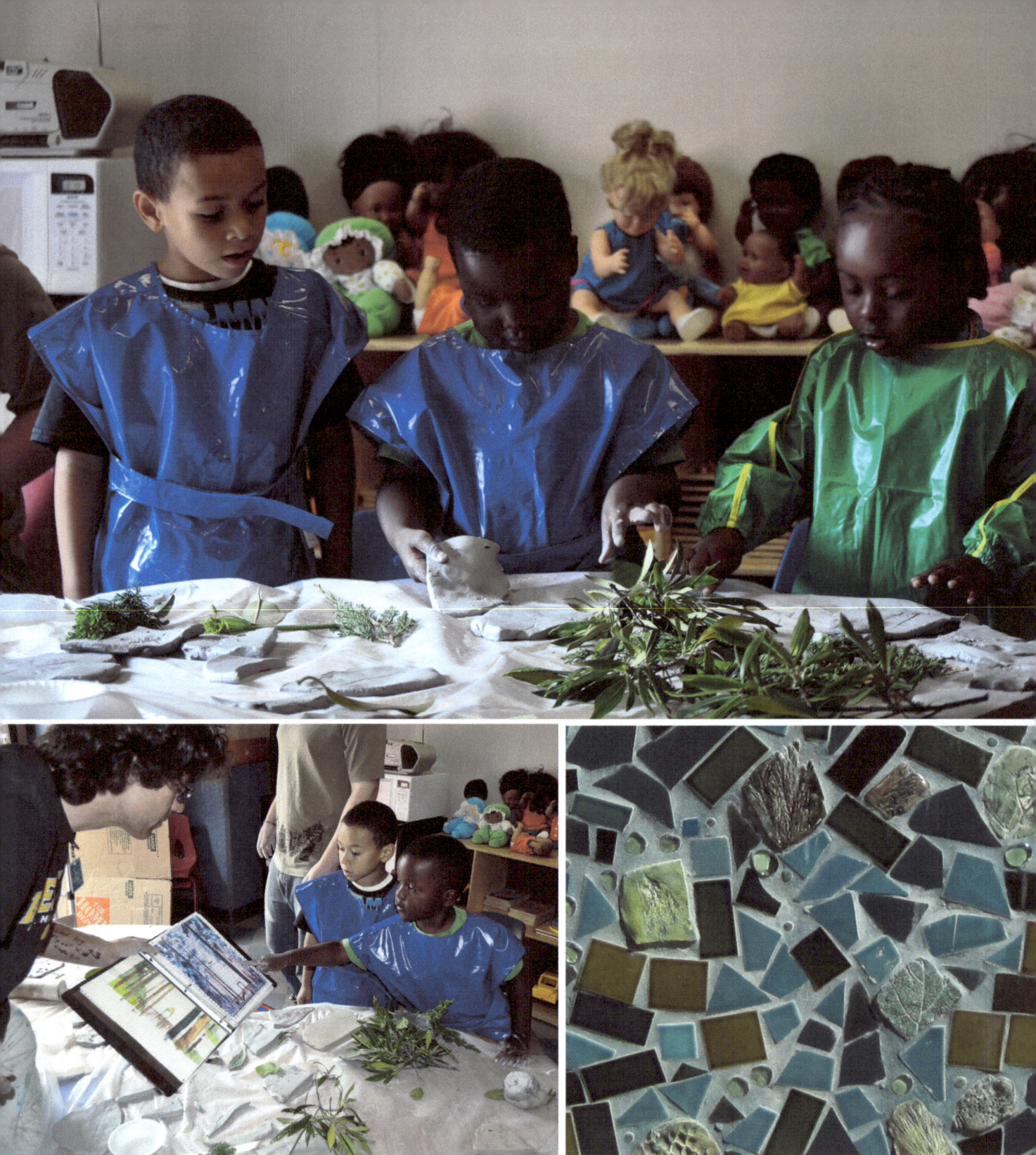

We also worked with younger artists at the Day Care located at 170 Otis Street. 4 year olds created leaf imprints into clay. These pieces were glazed, fired and installed on to the mural. Some of the kids came out to the site and helped build the lower part of the mural as well.

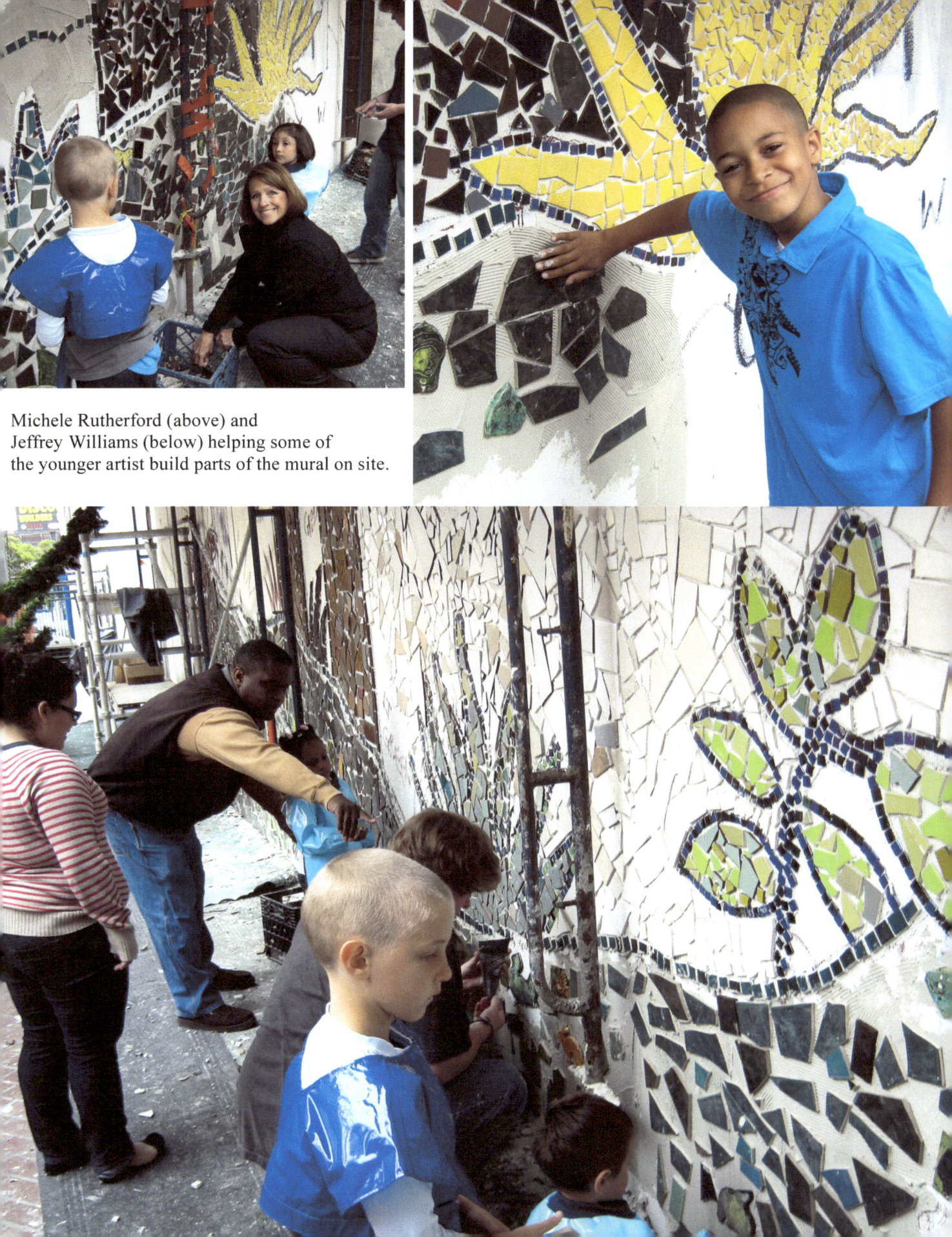

Michele Rutherford (above) and
Jeffrey Williams (below) helping some of
the younger artist build parts of the mural on site.

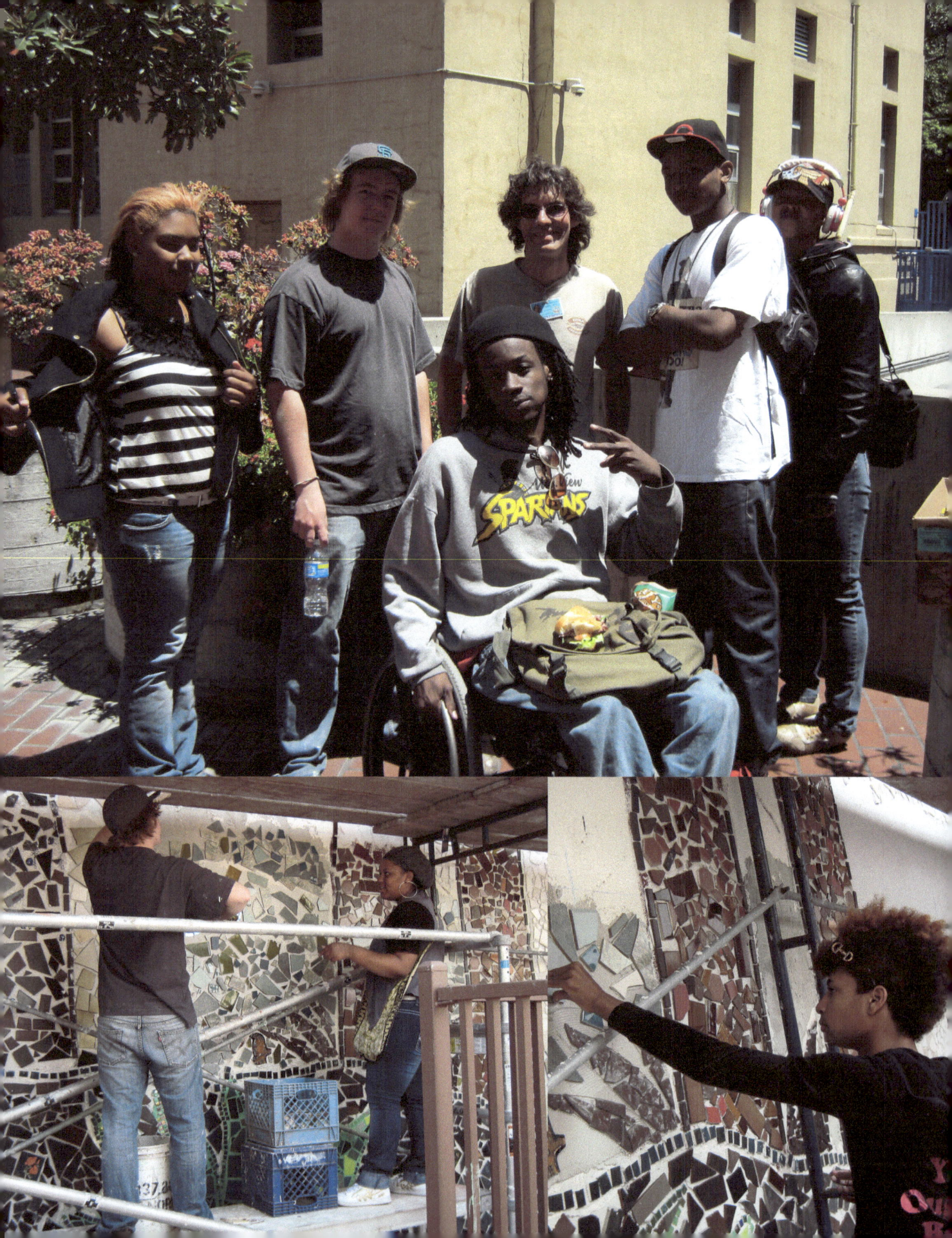

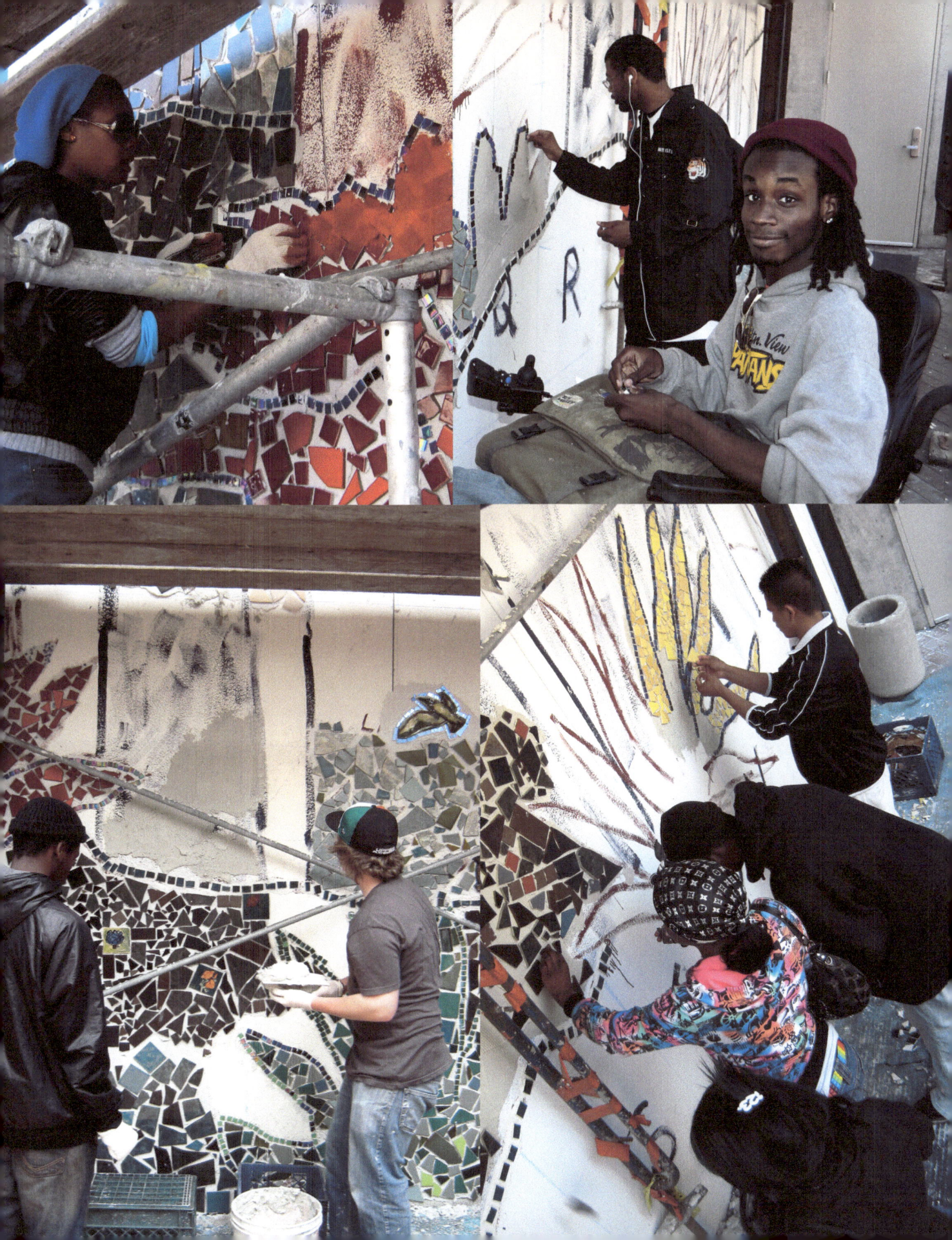

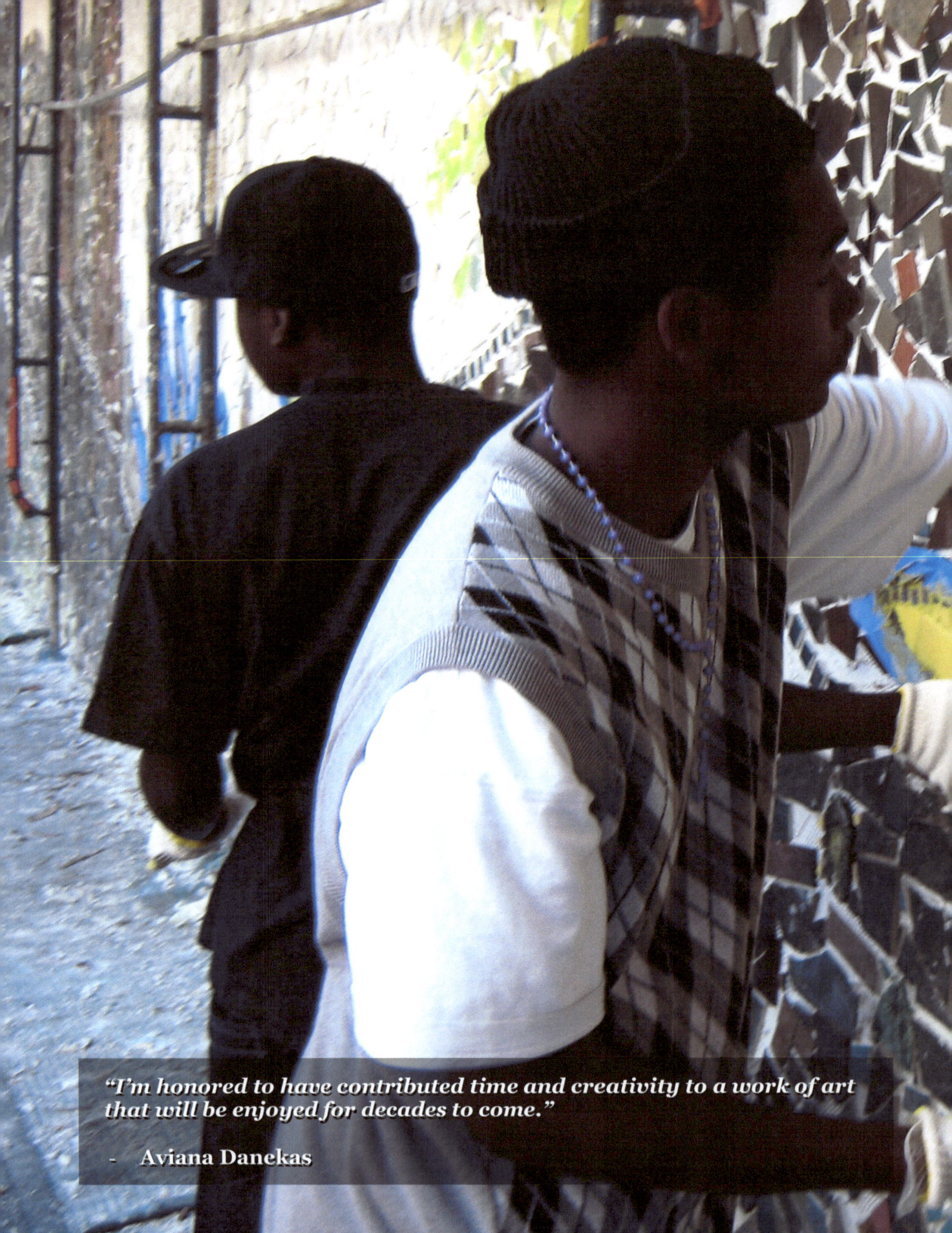

"I'm honored to have contributed time and creativity to a work of art that will be enjoyed for decades to come."

- Aviana Danekas

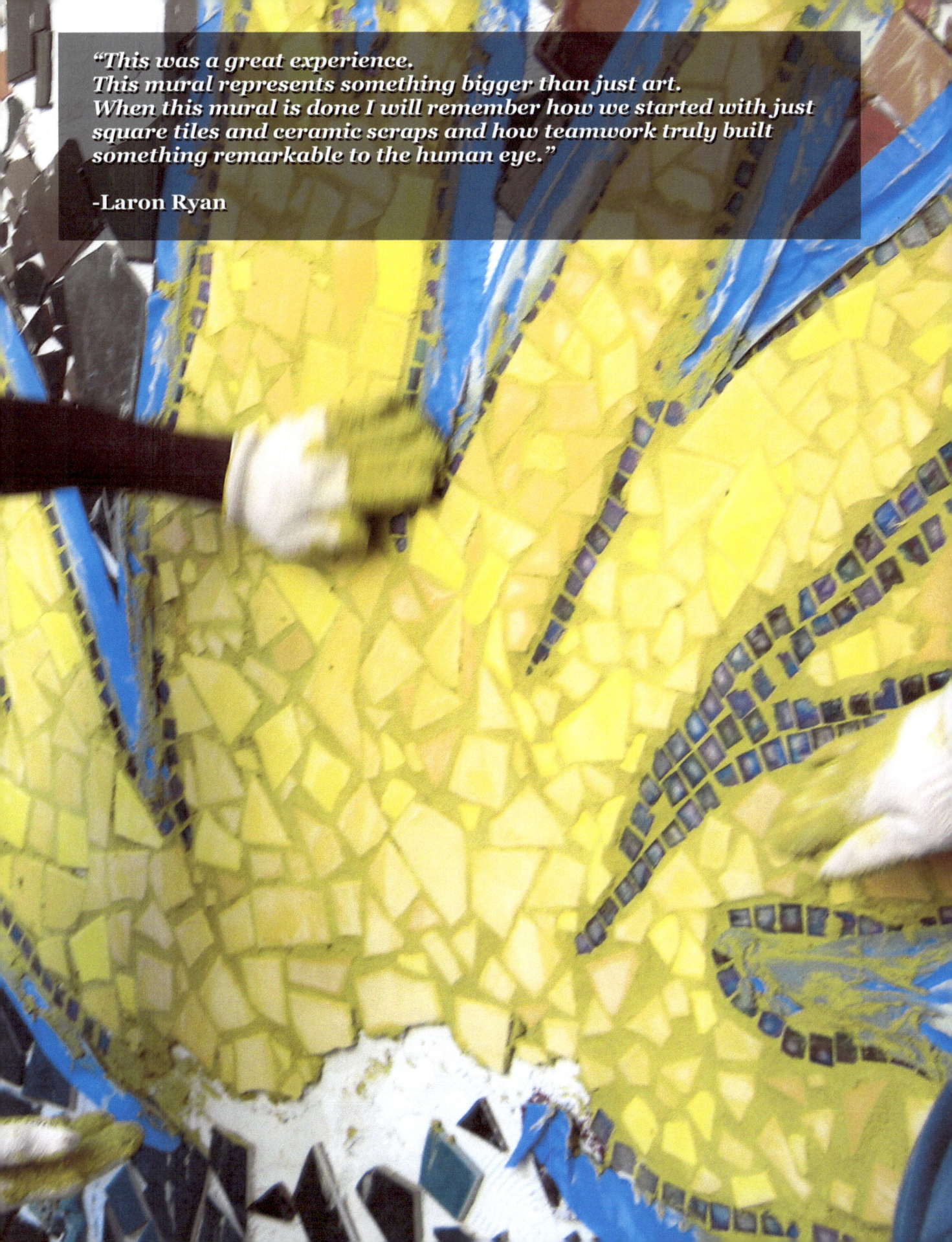

"*This was a great experience.*
This mural represents something bigger than just art.
When this mural is done I will remember how we started with just
square tiles and ceramic scraps and how teamwork truly built
something remarkable to the human eye."

-Laron Ryan

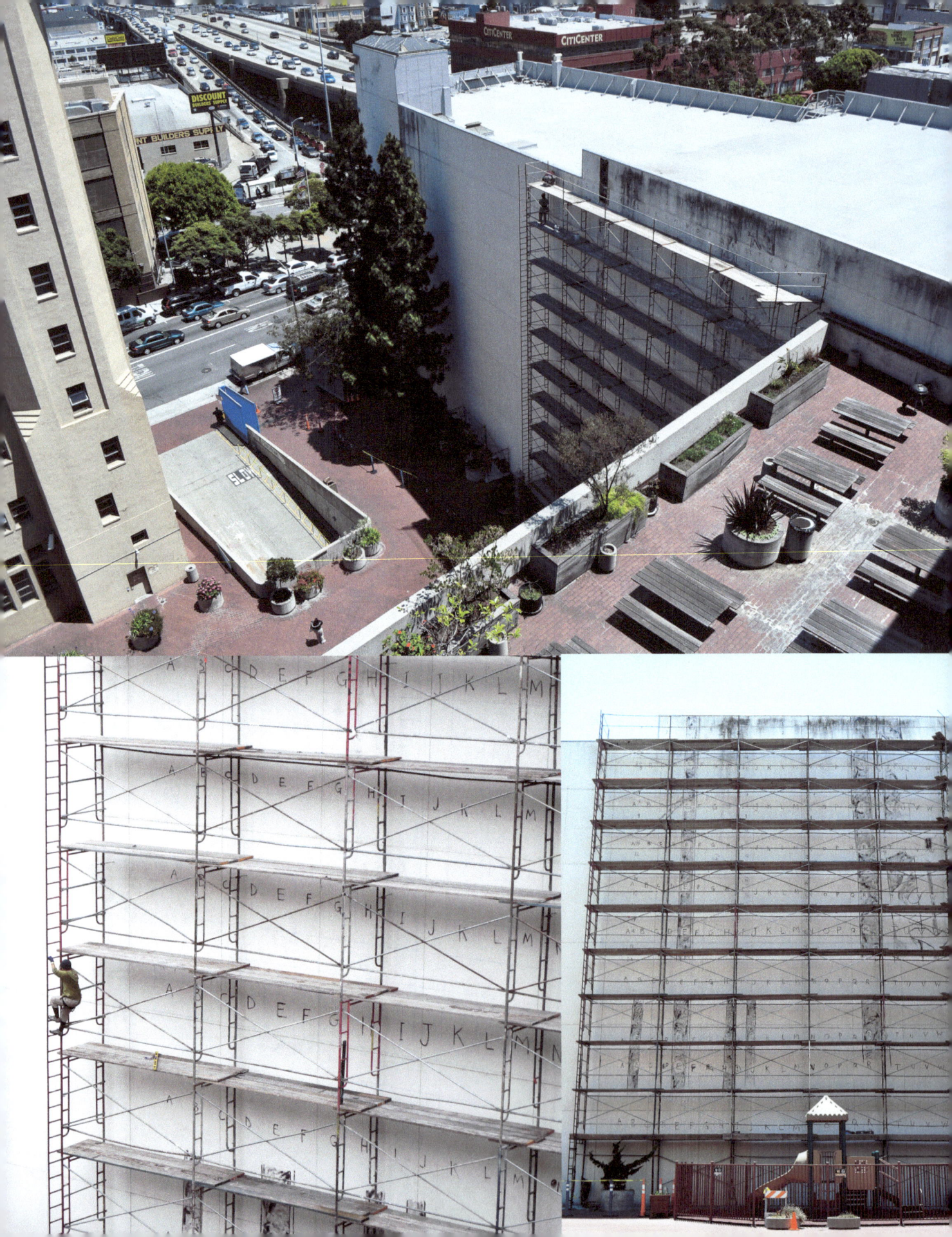

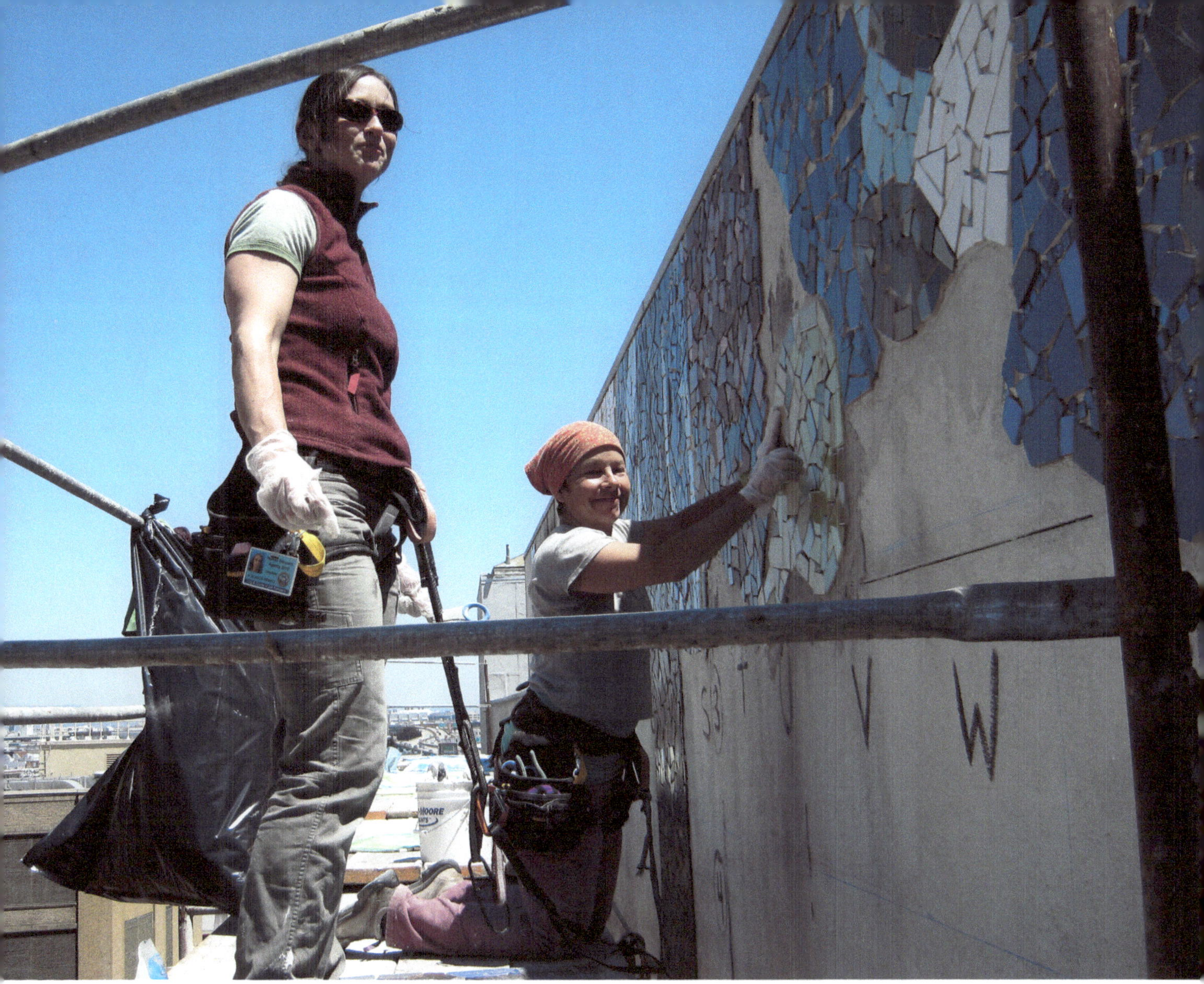

Installing a 2,000 square foot mosaic mural is an art form in itself. Atalanta Powell (left) and Delaine Hackney (right) installed the top half of the mural - 6 stories off the ground.

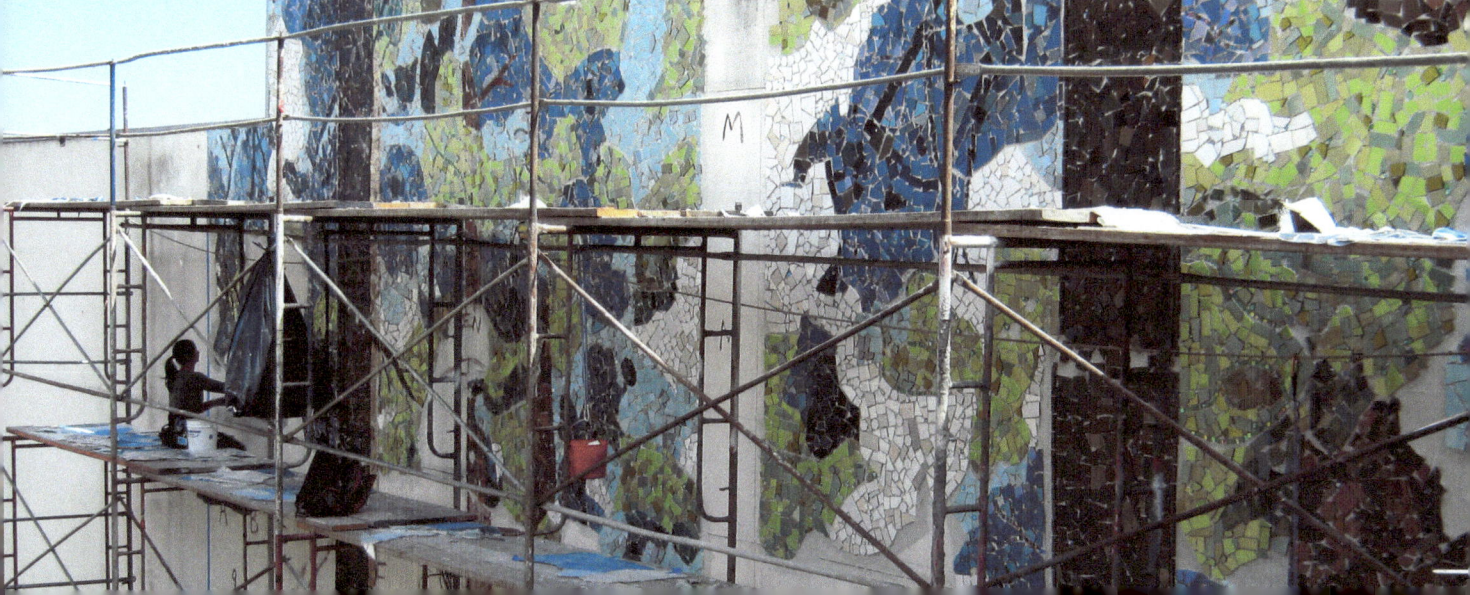

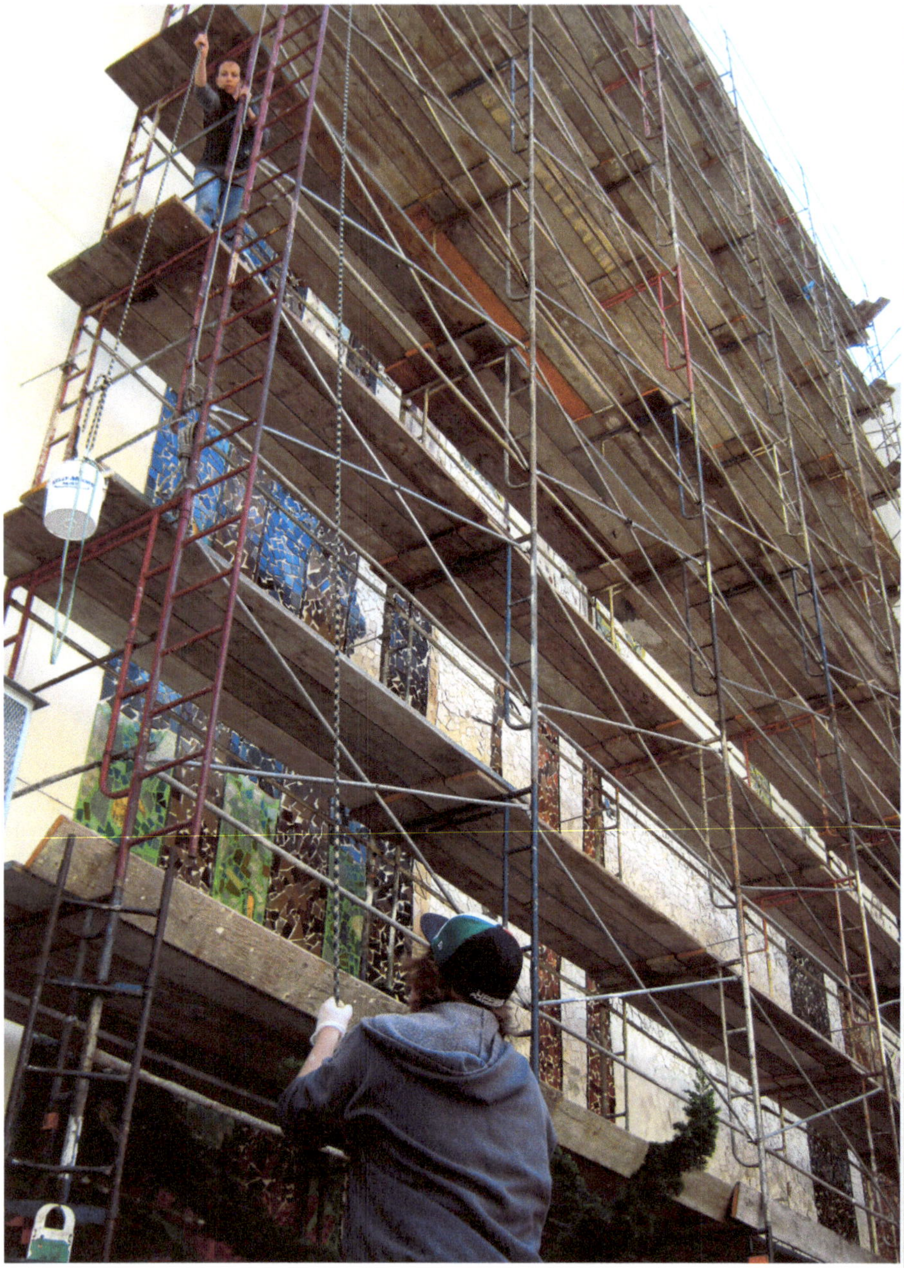

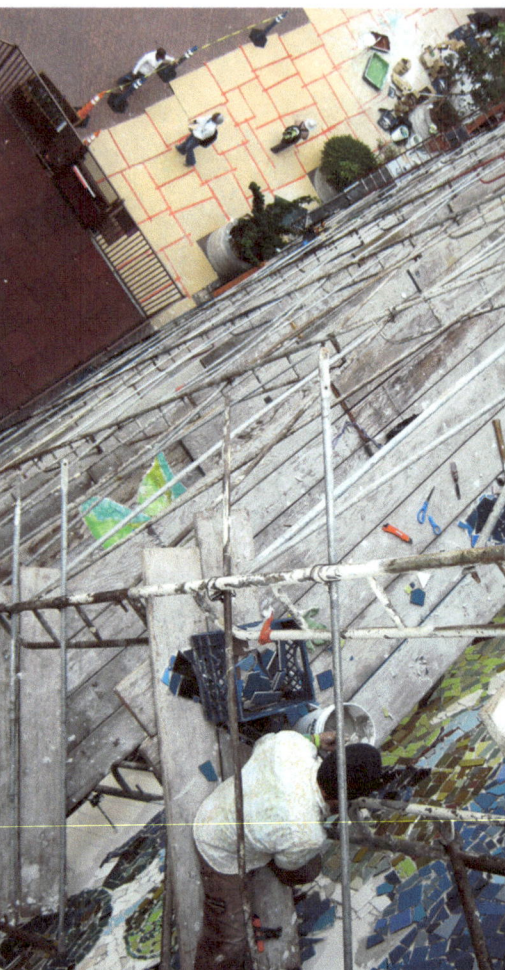

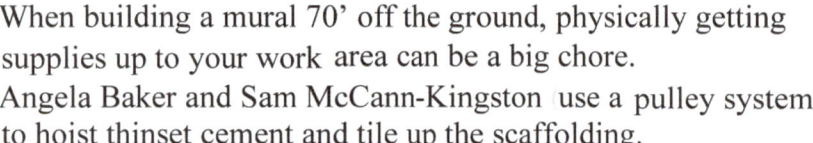

When building a mural 70' off the ground, physically getting supplies up to your work area can be a big chore.
Angela Baker and Sam McCann-Kingston use a pulley system to hoist thinset cement and tile up the scaffolding.

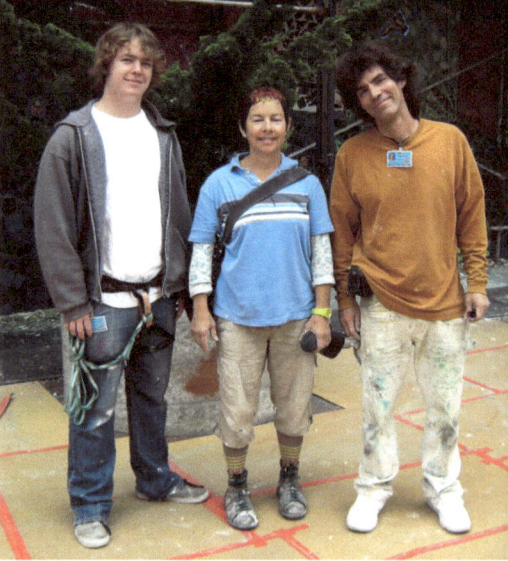

Sam McCann Kingston ,
Delaine Hackney and Josef Norris.

Sam McCann-Kingston had worked with Kid Serve previously as a high school intern.

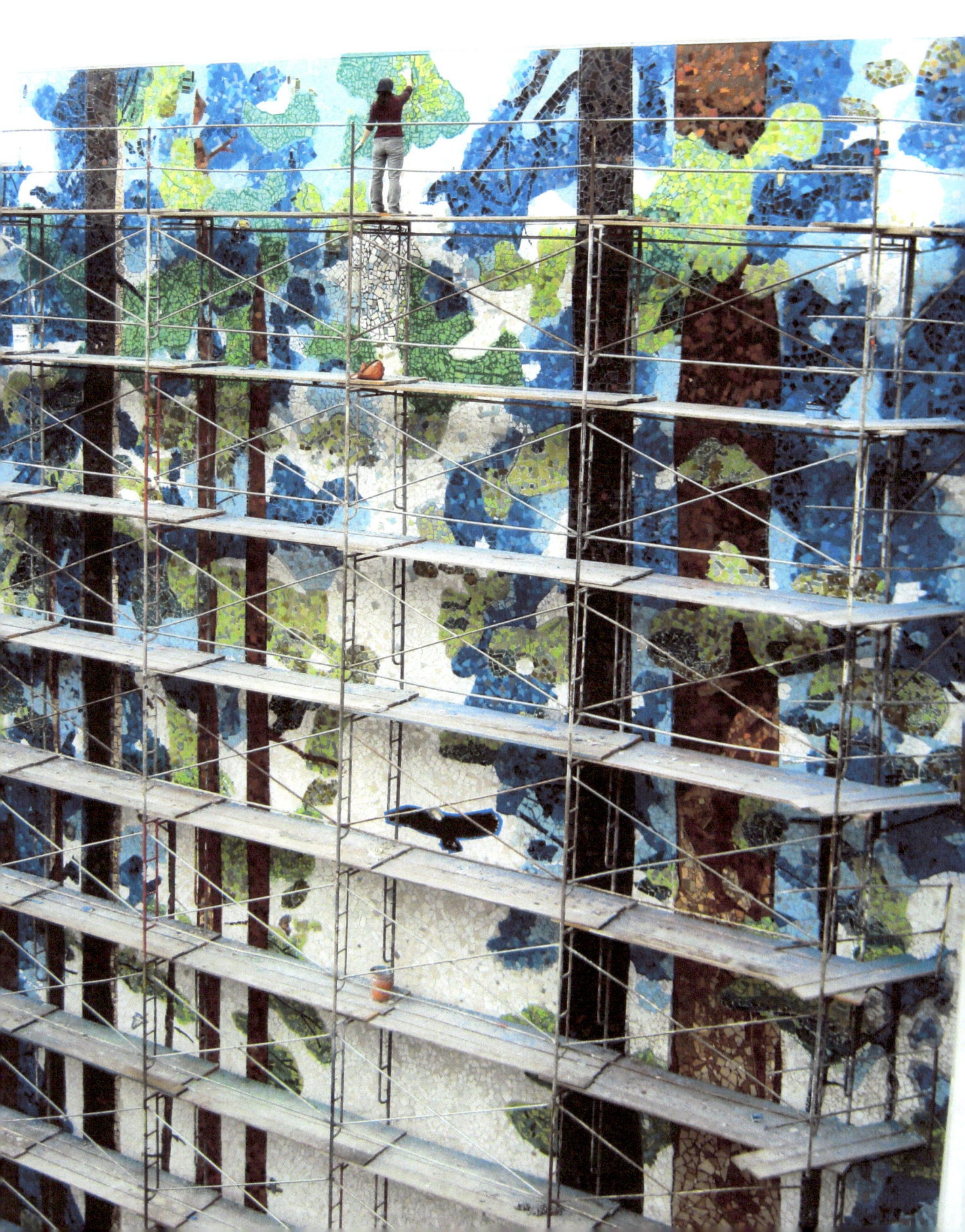

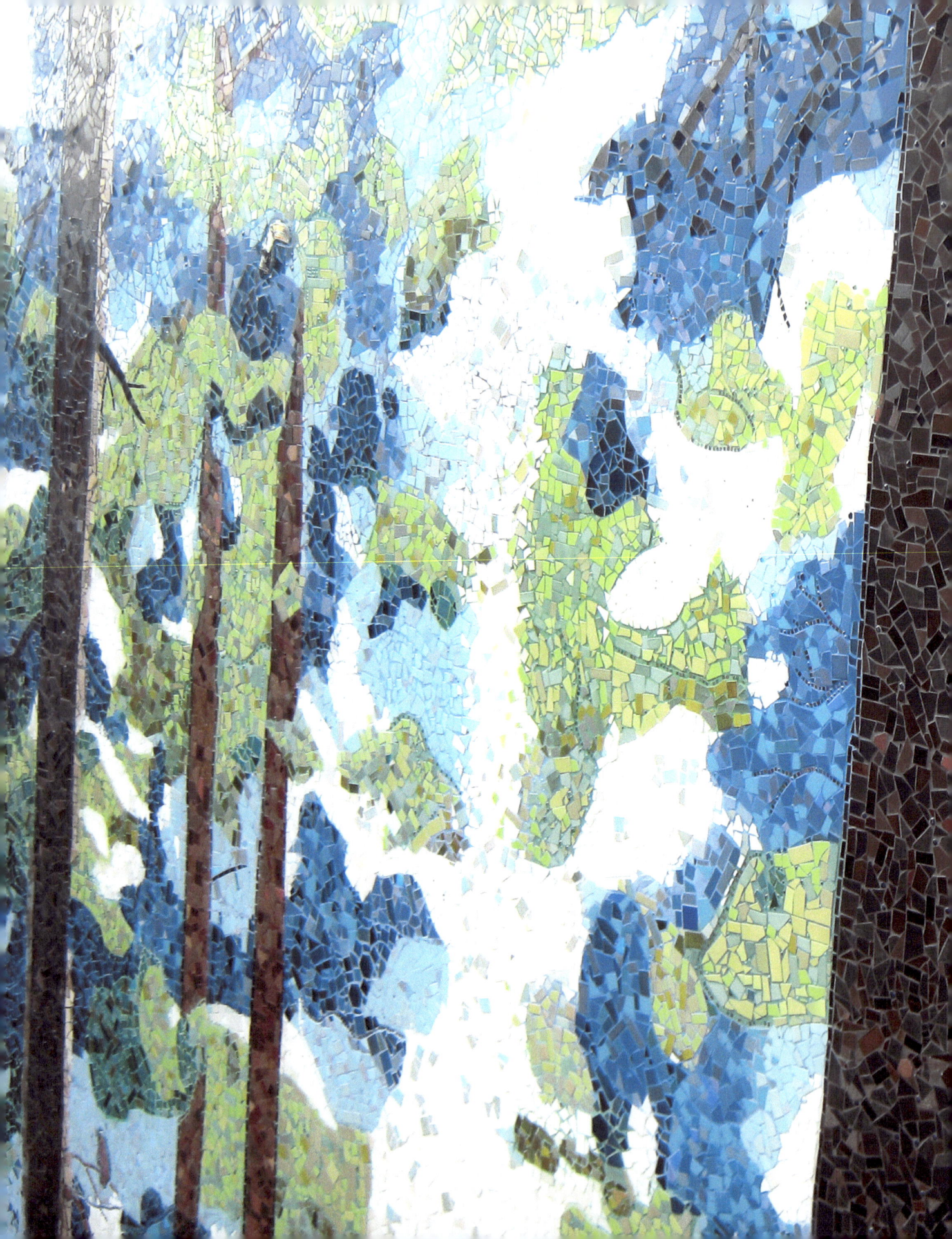

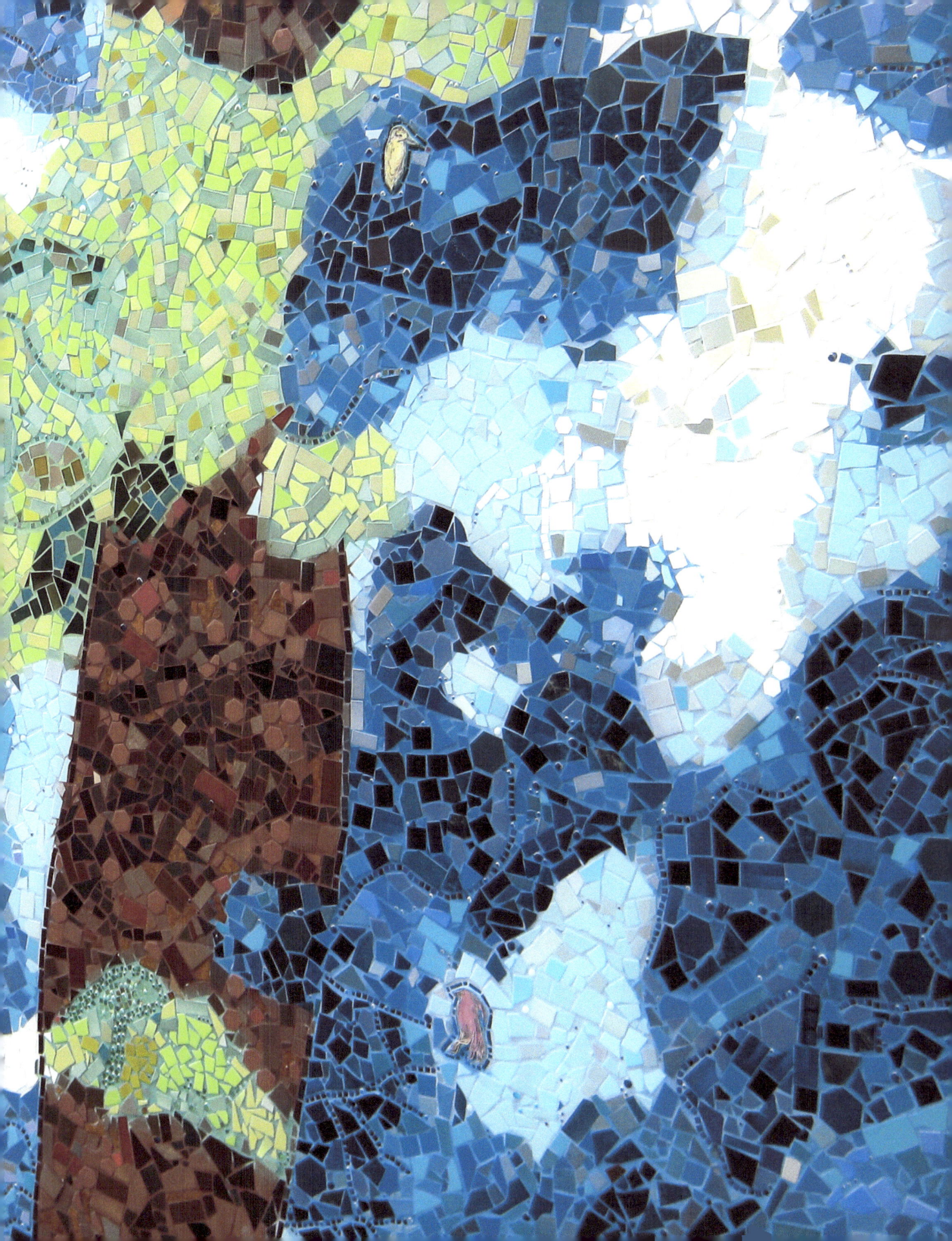

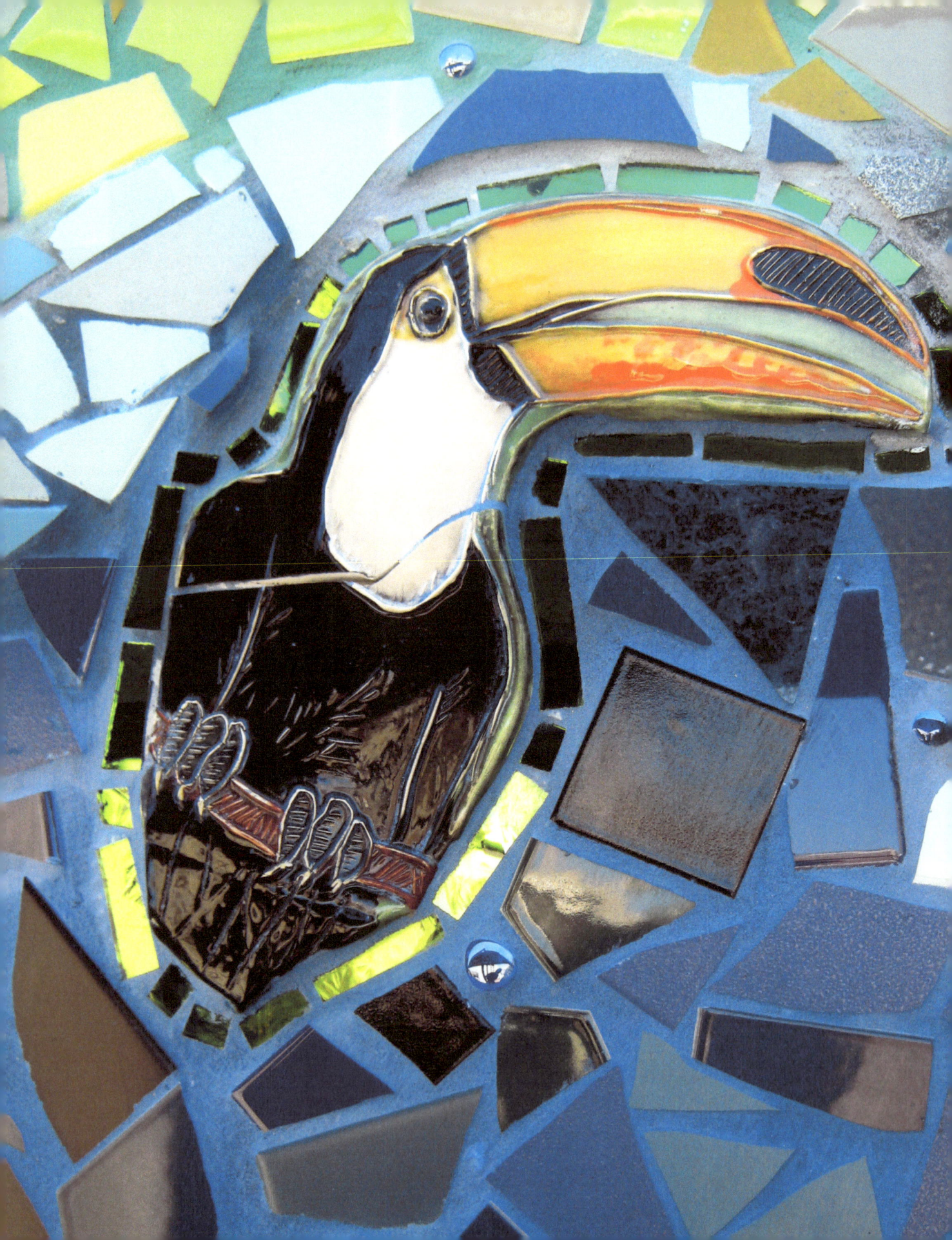

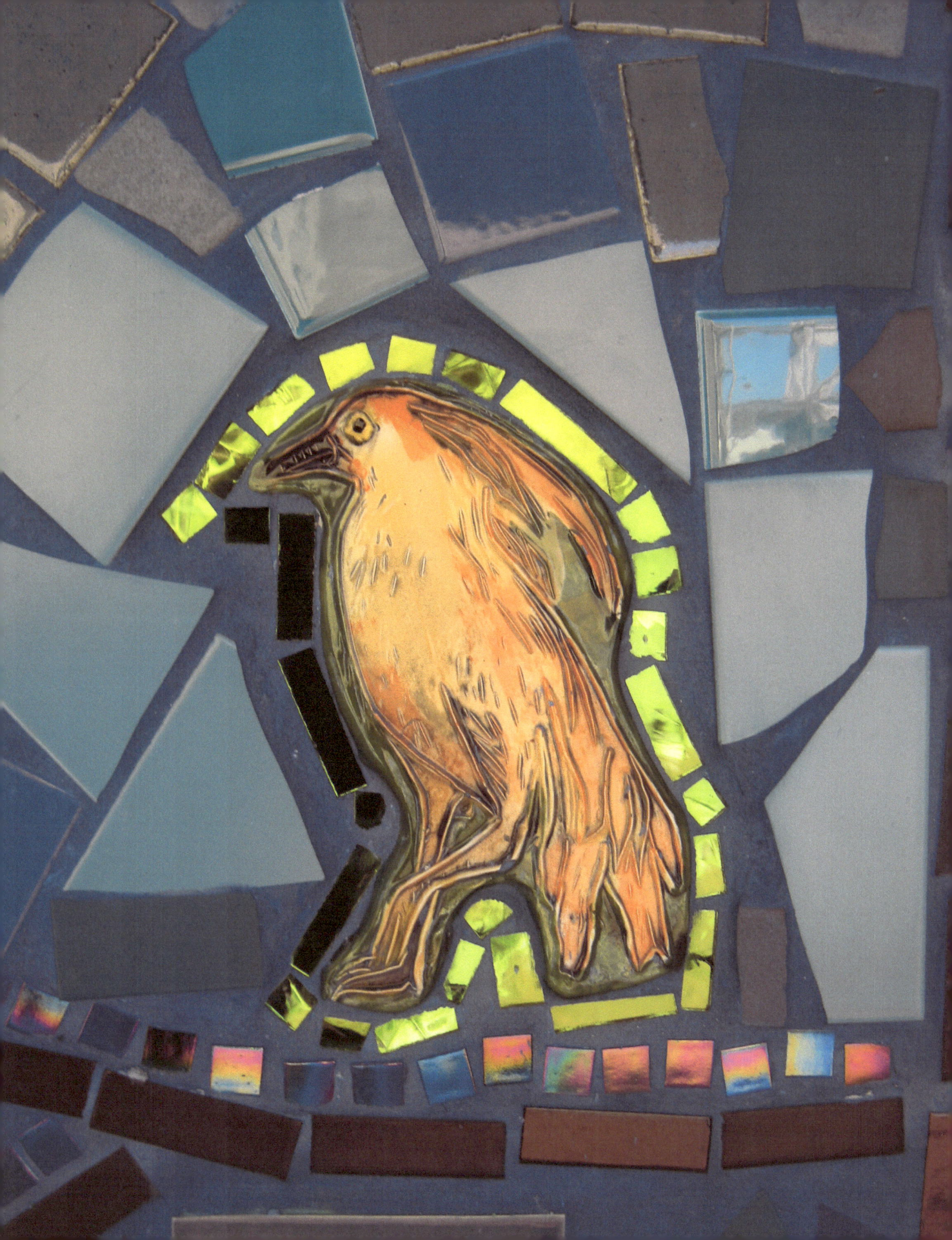

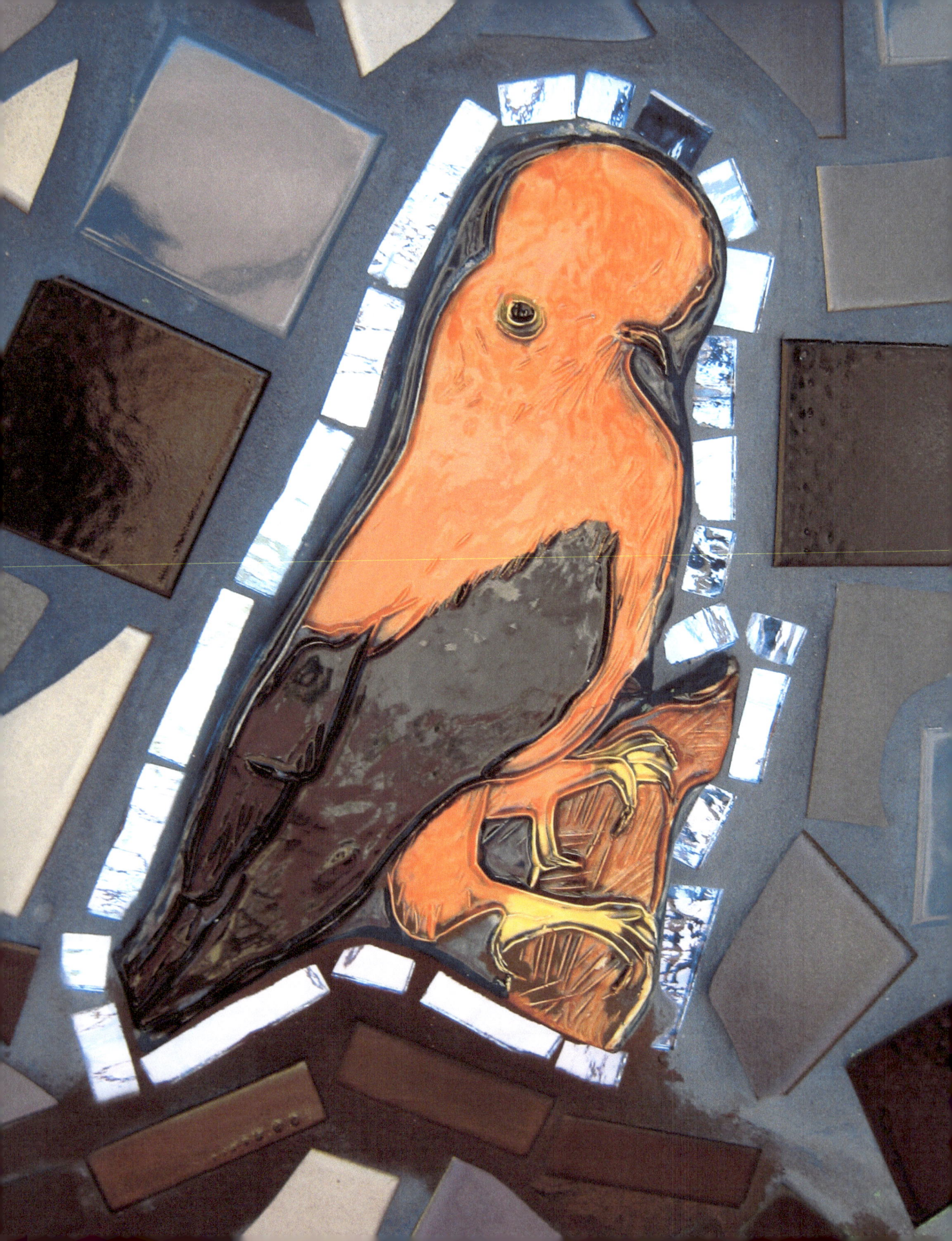

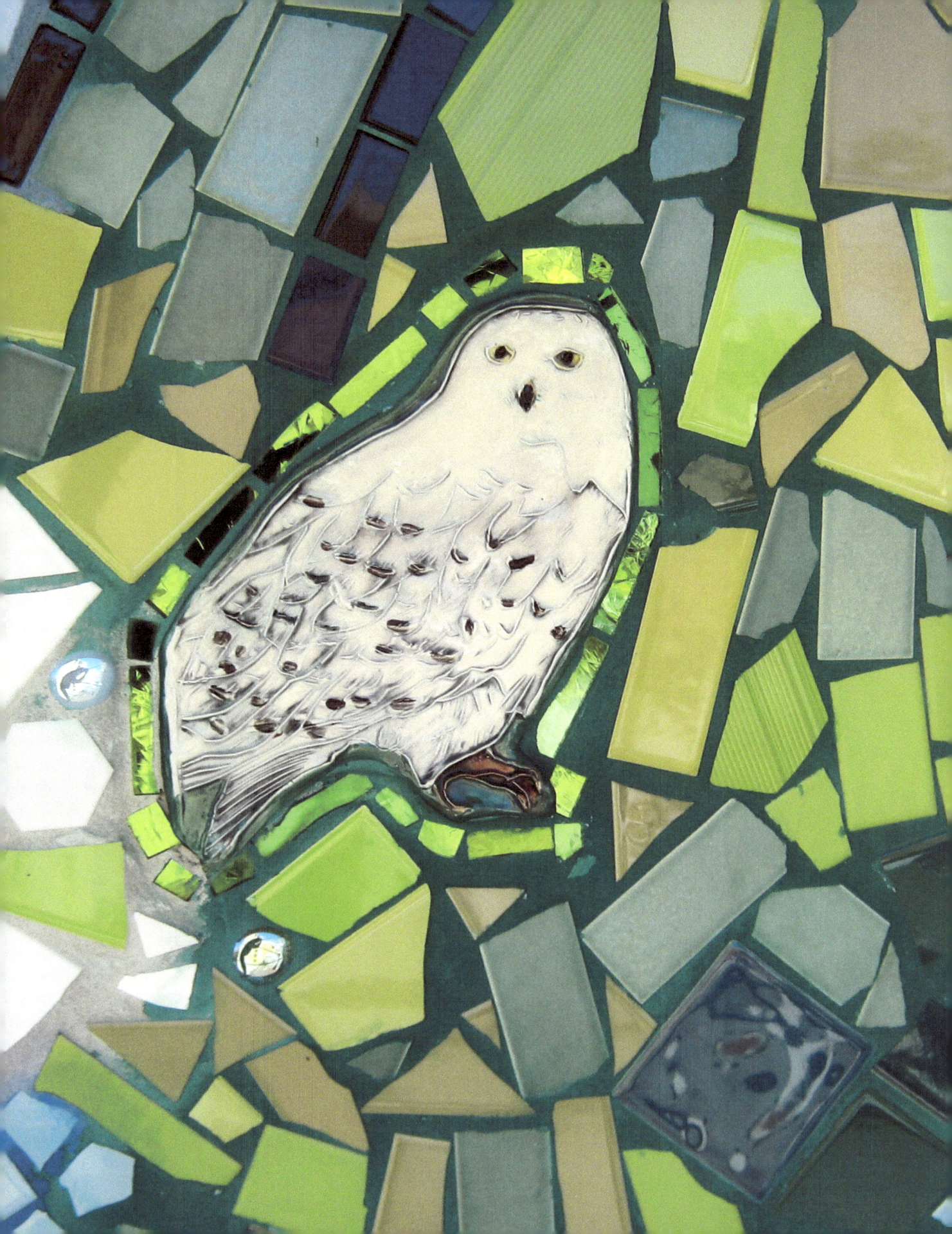

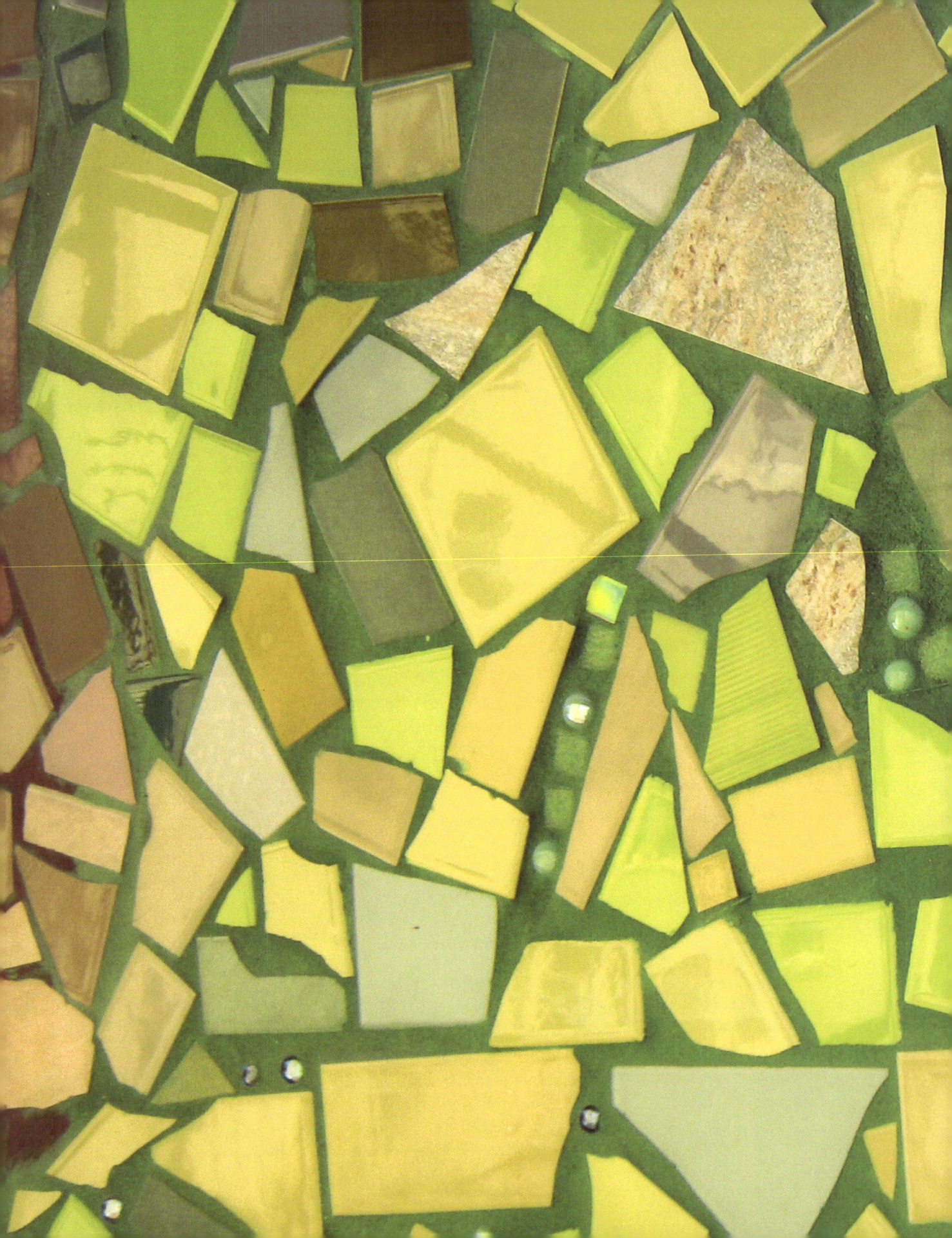

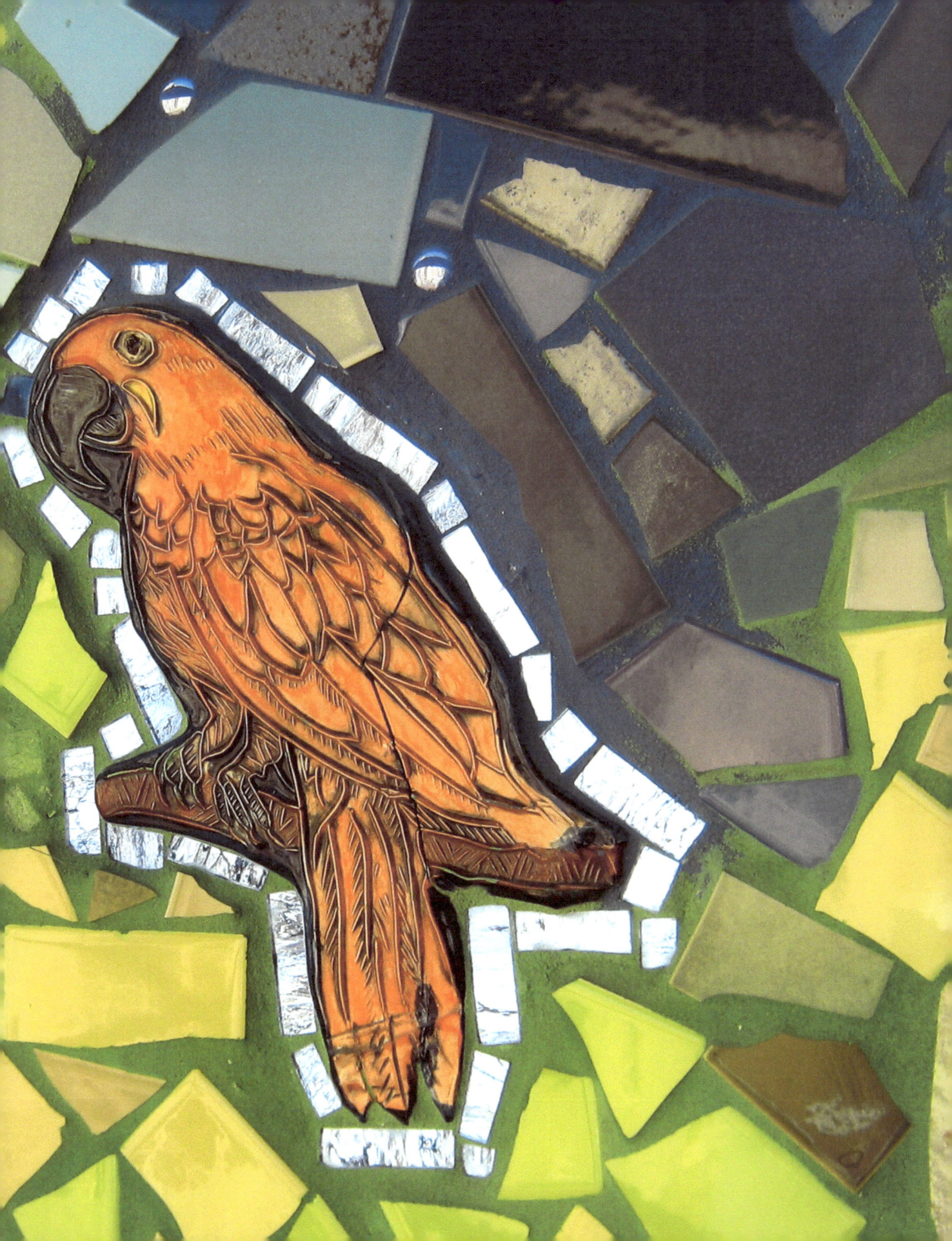

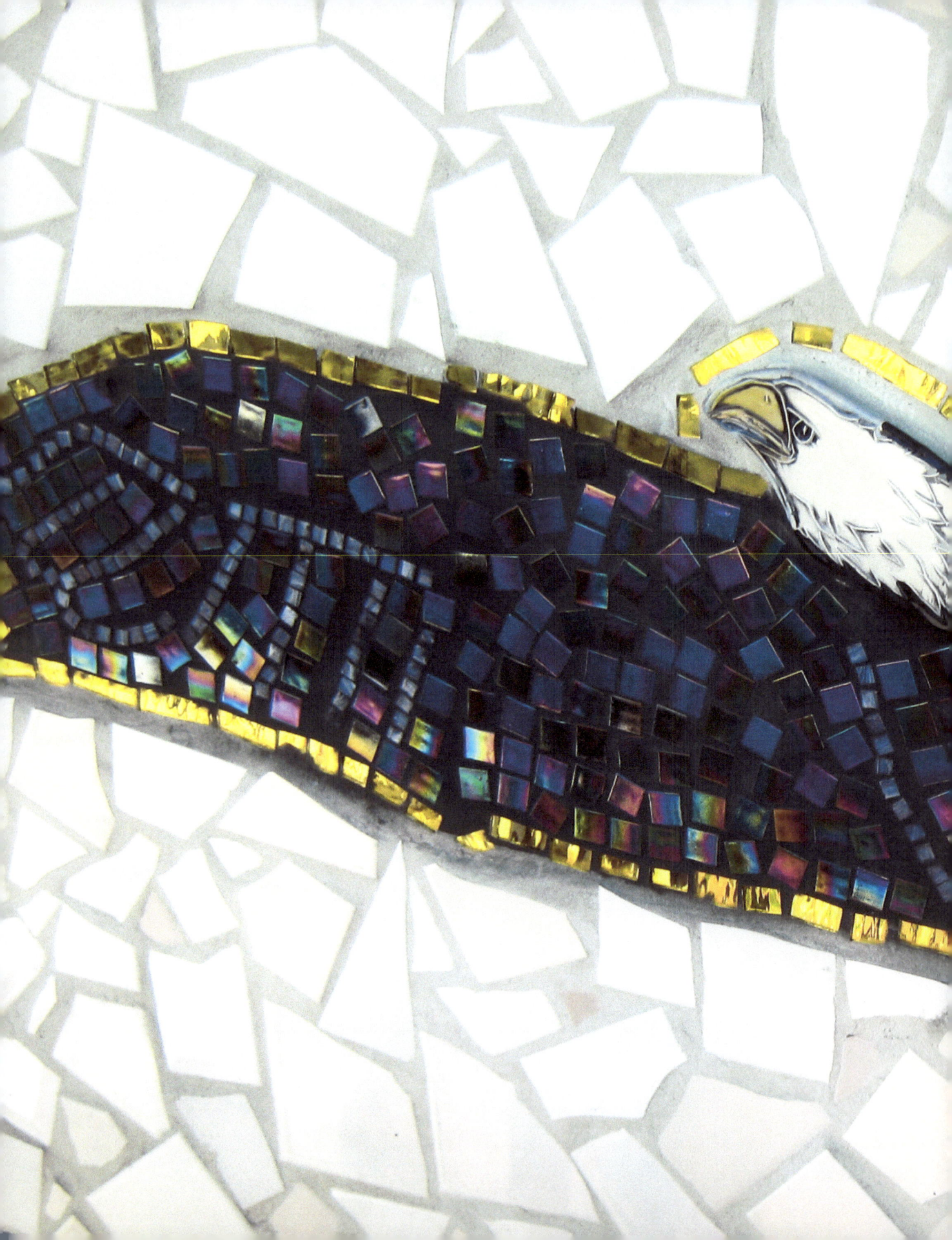

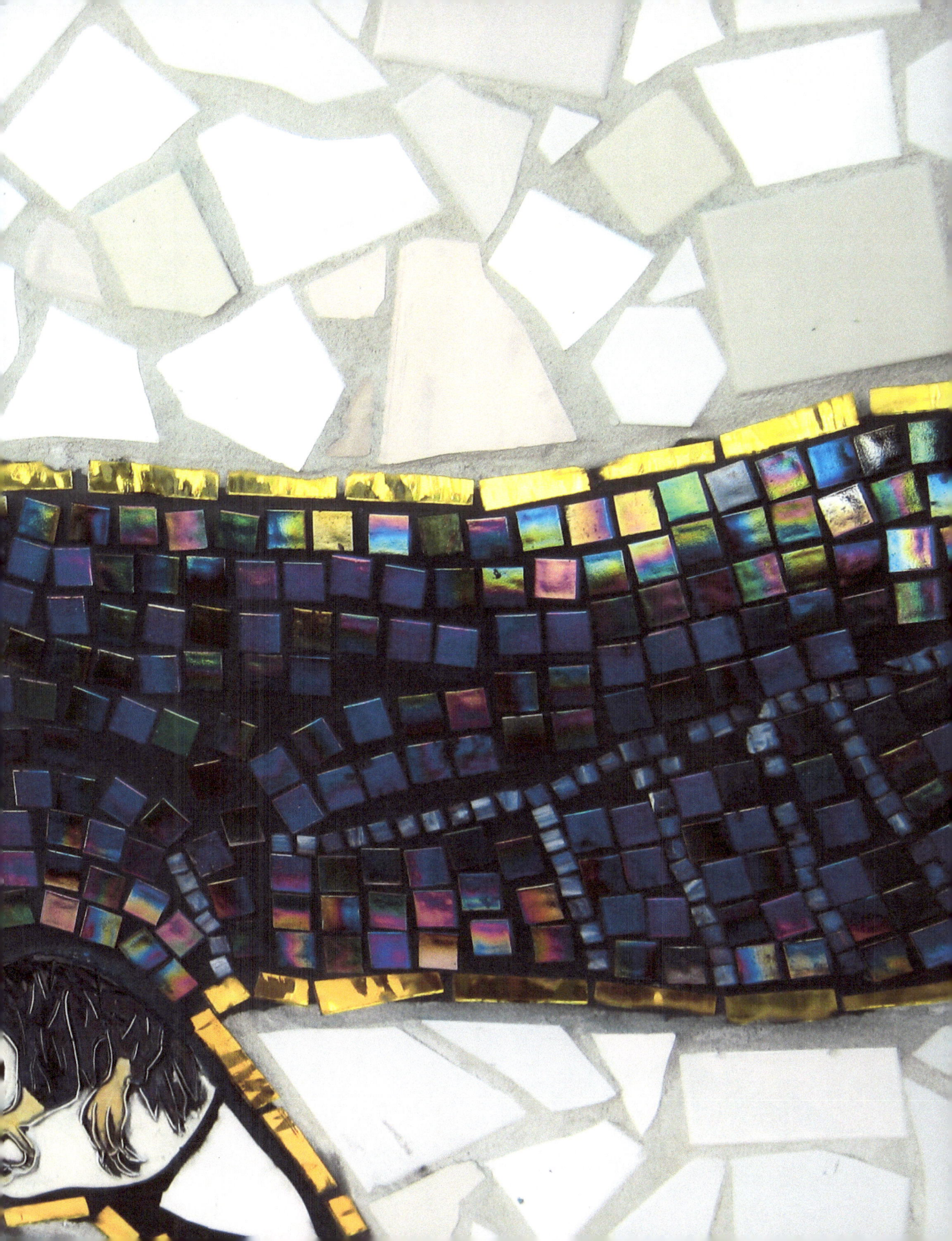

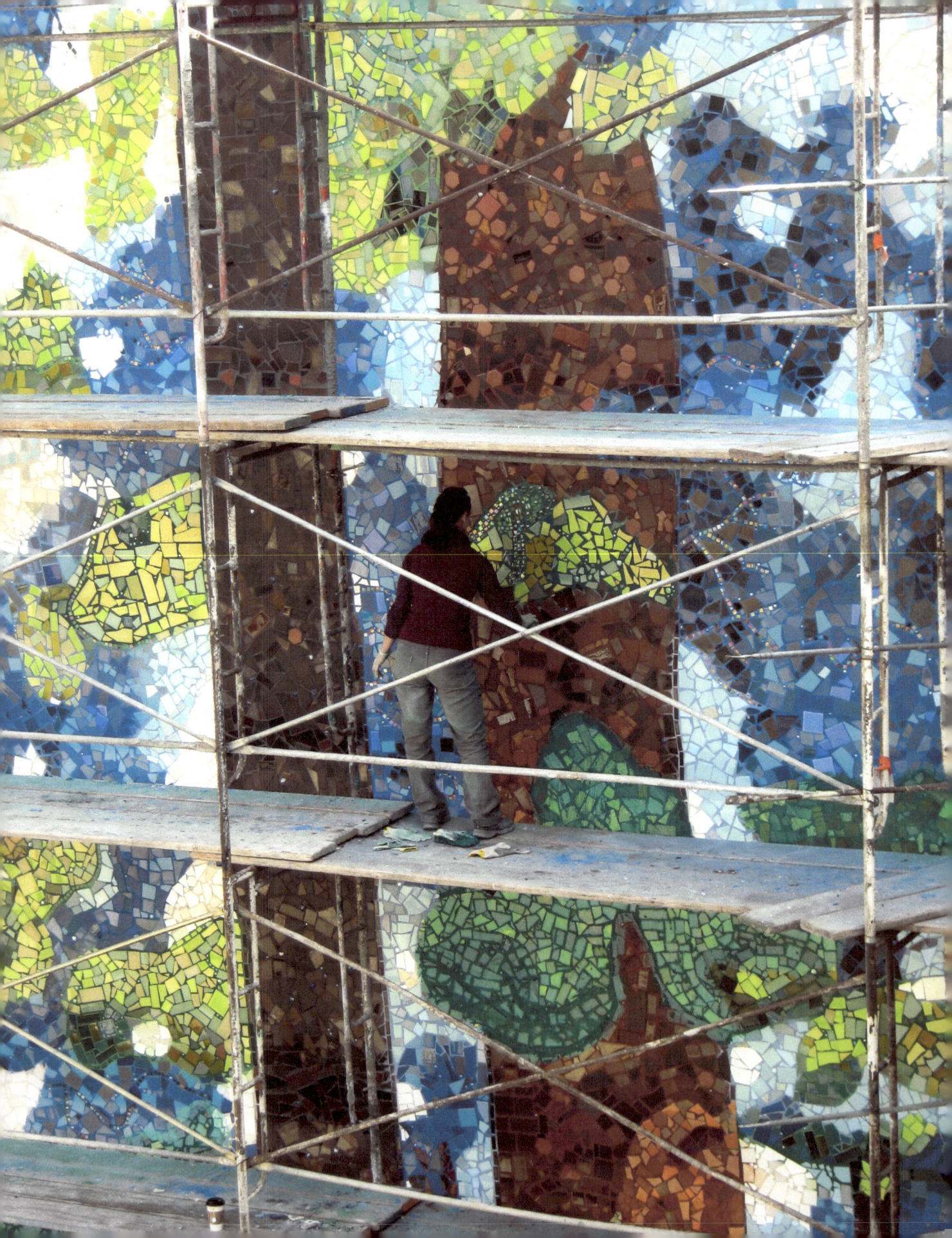

"BEYOND THE TREES"

by
Josef Norris

This is a project of
Kid Serve Youth Murals

Mural Assistants:

Atalanta Powell   Shakiri
Delaine Hackney   Sam McCann-Kingston
Angela Baker   Bashezo Nicole Boyd

Kid Serve Artists:

Lorall Hann   Stacey M. Jones
Aviana Danekas   Troyetta Carpenter
Elgin Rose   Joshua K. Ofakineiafu
Laron Marcel Ryan   Ian T. Smith
Pepito Jackson   Valerie SeuSeu
Marcelino Paxtor Chay   Laronda Johnson
Lovely E. Rosemon   Jazmin Ford
Clariyon Clark   Kelvin Richardson
Ardelia Lewis

Made possible by a grant from:
San Francisco Arts Commission
Arts and Communities: Innovative Partnerships – Realization Grant
The Starbucks Foundation Youth Action Grant
The Zellerbach Family Foundation
And many Individual Donors

This is a partnership with
Intersection for the Arts, The City of San Francisco Human Services
Agency, Independent Living Skills Program of San Francisco
and the Worker's Children Fund

Special Thanks to:
Trent Rhorer, E.D., Michele Rutherford, Nancy Bliss, Jeffrey Williams,
Storage Advantage Self Storage, Arlene Hylton, Idries Aziz-Pearson,
Steve Nelson and all the instructors at I.L.S.P. San Francisco and the
Kid Serve Board of Directors

This mural is dedicated to
HSA Commissioner George Yamisaki and his wife, Anne
for their long-term support of HSA and foster youth

Josef Norris is a self-taught artist who has created over 100 murals in San Francisco. Josef is the founder and director of Kid Serve Youth Murals, an arts education program that guides children in schools through the process of creating permanent murals in their neighborhood. He lives in San Francisco with his wife and son.

Josef Norris' work can be seen on his website at: **www.josefnorris.com**
Kid Serve Youth Murals can be reached at: **www.kidserve.com**